"I FELT

Does the name D̶ you?

Dr. Conant authored a book, **"Every Member Evangelism,"** which fell into my hands in the early days of my seminary training. It inflamed me. God used it to stir me for the cause of **personal** Christianity.

That is part of the story.

The day came when Dr. Conant heard of my efforts and invited me to come and see him. We met. Instantly the Holy Spirit knitted our hearts in wondrous fellowship. We rejoiced before the Lord as we talked of His call upon our lives. I came away thrilled with the privilege of meeting this great man of God.

Then a letter came. Dr. Conant said he must see me as soon as possible. I went. With shaking emotion he told me there was one thing he must do before his house would be in order. At that moment, he was dying of cancer and his heart was burdened for a successor to carry on the program.

One of the overwhelming moments of my life arrived. This giant of God put his arm about my shoulder and with tears streaming down his face, said . . .

"Brother Lovett, I pass my mantle on to you!"

This was his last act for Jesus. Shortly after that he passed into the presence of his Master.

Now you know the source of my burden. The Holy Spirit sealed that act to my soul and I wear that mantle today. Within me burns an aching passion to see every Christian unashamed of Jesus and equipped to exalt Him openly. If some of this burden shifts to you as you read, then you will not be satisfied until your work is reaching souls for our Lord Jesus Christ.

C.S. Lovett

ABOUT THE AUTHOR. . .DR. C. S. LOVETT

Dr. Lovett is the president of **Personal Christianity,** a fundamental, evangelical interdenominational ministry. For the past 27 years he has had but one objective—**preparing Christians for the second coming of Christ!** This book is one of over 35 of his works designed to help believers be **prepared for His appearing.**

Dr. Lovett's decision to serve the Lord resulted in the loss of a sizable personal fortune. He is well equipped for the job the Lord has given him. A graduate of California Baptist Theological Seminary, he holds the M.A. and B.D. degrees conferred *Magna Cum Laude.* He has also completed graduate work in psychology at Los Angeles State College and holds an honorary doctorate from the Protestant Episcopal University in London.

A retired Air Force Chaplain (Lt. Colonel), he has been married to Marjorie for over 36 years and has two grown daughters dedicated to the Lord.

SOUL-WINNING MADE EASY

THE ENCOUNTER-METHOD

by C. S. Lovett

M.A., B.D., D.D.

president of Personal Christianity

author of eleven best selling books including:

Dealing With The Devil
Witnessing Made Easy
Jesus Wants You Well!
"Help Lord—The Devil Wants Me Fat!"

ILLUSTRATED BY LINDA LOVETT

CHRIST AT THE DOOR
cover painting by Linda Lovett

published by:
PERSONAL CHRISTIANITY
Box 549
Baldwin Park, California 91706

Dedicated to

WARREN E. BELKNAP

whose dedicated skills and loving
encouragements have meant so much to
the author and advanced the ministry
of **Personal Christianity.**

PRINTED IN THE UNITED STATES OF AMERICA

by
EL CAMINO PRESS
La Verne, California 91750

Contents

"I Felt Like Elisha. . .!" 1

About The Author 2

Introduction—How It All Began 7

PART ONE—Your Soul-Winning Plan

Chapter One—Your Soul-Winning Plan 14

Chapter Two—The Tools You'll Need 27

Chapter Three—Some Hints That Help 34

Chapter Four—The X-Ray Approach Technique . . 44

Chapter Five—Presenting Christ Alive! 53

Chapter Six—How To Press For The Decision . . . 78

Chapter Seven—Presenting The Booklets 88

PART TWO—Using Your Soul-Winning Plan

Chapter Eight—Learning The Plan 98

Chapter Nine—Psychology And The Soul-
Winner 116

Chapter Ten—Do I Have To Try To Win Everybody?. 124

Chapter Eleven—Too Scared To Try? 132

The tour of Personal Christianity stops at this showcase (above). Through the glass you can see the very first copy of the soul-winning plan mimeographed in 1951 (below). On either side are the first two printed editions.

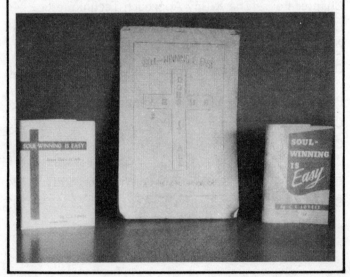

How It All Began

---

*"Within our community God has appointed, in the
first place apostles, in the second place prophets,
thirdly teachers; then miracle-workers, then those who
have gifts of healing, or ability to help others or
power to guide them, or the gift of ecstatic utterance
of various kinds."* (1 Cor. 12:28 NEB)

Were you to visit **Personal Christianity** and take a tour
of our facilities, the tour would begin in front of a glass
display case in our chapel foyer. The tour guide would
say . . . "This is where it all began." As you look through
the glass all you see is a faded, green syllabus. On the
well-worn cover, you make out the words . . . SOUL-
WINNING IS EASY . . . JESUS DOES IT ALL! There's
a date, too . . . **1951.**

That rings a bell. You've heard that title before. If you
are familiar with our ministry, you know it was the first
book the Lord led me to write. But how is that book
connected with this syllabus?

In 1951 I entered the California Baptist Theological
Seminary. The Lord had called me to preach the gospel.

Yet, if I were going to be a preacher, I needed a place to preach. So in that same year, the Lord also led me to establish the Baldwin Park Baptist Church. In this way I could work with the truths I was learning. I was 34 years old then.

My professor of evangelism, Dr. John Pre Vol, a blessed servant of the Lord, took me out onto the streets and showed me how to approach people with the Word of God. But since my training in evangelism consisted mostly of scripture memorization, I didn't have much success in bringing people to Jesus. In time, though, the Lord opened a way for me to minister in the jails and finally to become a chaplain at the huge Los Angeles County General Hospital.

Now I was able to get lots of experience dealing with people who cared nothing for the frills of religion, but longed to be saved. In the process of working with thousands on a **MAN TO MAN** basis, the Holy Spirit brought forth a unique method of winning souls. It brought people swiftly to the place where they had to **DO SOMETHING** with Jesus. Nearly everyone I would deal with made a clear cut decision . . . either for Jesus or against Him. The plan was extremely successful.

What I had **really** discovered was **HOW TO WORK WITH THE HOLY SPIRIT** in confronting men with Christ. The method was simple, easy to use. It was based on the faithfulness of the Holy Spirit to make Jesus real, rather than on my cleverness. I only needed four Scripture verses.

The people of my church became aware of my success as a soul-winner and asked me to share the method with them. So our first piece of literature was this mimeographed syllabus containing the plan the Spirit had given me. We made up 100 of them. The one you see on the tour is the very first one.

As different ones read the plan and tried it, they found they could win souls. You can imagine the fever that spread. The church began to grow. It had to.

The following year, 1952, God sent Warren Belknap to us. You'll note this book is dedicated to him. He came with some printing skills. At his urging, we printed our mimeographed plan in a small book, keeping the same title. With different ones of the church helping, we made up 8000 copies. That seemed ambitious at the time. But we didn't know what God had in mind. As these were offered to individuals and pastors at $1.00 each, they went like hot cakes. Before long we were receiving letters from people all over, telling how they had won their first souls to Jesus.

We had sampled the power of books!

That gave me a different vision of the ministry. I realized that God had shown me a powerful way to help His people. It was at that point that I shifted our church into gear as a **"ministry of helps"** (I Cor. 12:28). The congregation committed itself to a literature ministry. Once our vision began to encompass the whole family of believers, we could no longer call ourselves the Baldwin Park Baptist Church. We chose the name **Personal Christianity,** because we wanted to help our brethren and get them personally involved with the Holy Spirit and the Great Commission.

After another year had passed, Warren took the money that he had saved for a new car, and used it to buy a small press. That was the kick-off of our literature ministry. At first he would do the printing in his garage at night after work. But when the nights got too cold, his wife, Elenore, consented to let him bring the press into the house. Whenever I would go to their house for dinner, I could look across the dining room table and see it. Yes—it was in the living room! Now that is some kind of a sacrifice. You can see why this book is dedicated to him.

Here is Warren in his garage with our first press in 1953.

The results produced by the soul-winning book were so good, the demand was increasing. In time we came to see how this method really focuses on the **ENCOUNTER** with Christ. So we began referring to it as the **EN-COUNTER-METHOD OF SOUL-WINNING.**

Now you understand how the ministry of **Personal Christianity** began—with a book—**this book.** We never dreamed that from this little syllabus would come a book that is now serving as the standard evangelism text in countless Bible schools, colleges and churches around the world. There couldn't be a more humble beginning.

If you learn this method as I've laid it out for you, you won't be disappointed. You'll be thrilled to discover, as I did, just how much the Holy Spirit does for you. Yes, you'll feel clumsy at first. That's true of anything new we try. But get that first soul under your belt, and you'll be on your way as a lifetime soul-winner.

This knowledge is powerful, for it shows you how to take advantage of the Holy Spirit's ministry. He does many things of which the average soul-winner is not aware. Gradually you'll come to see that your part is quite small and that He is the real soul-winner. When the reality of His work grips you, you will thrill to the supernatural. From then on, the greatest joy of your life will be presenting Christ . . .

. . . ALIVE!

C. S. Lovett, 1978

THE ENCOUNTER-METHOD

Jesus
Is
Alive

Since the Holy Spirit makes Him real, men can meet Jesus in a dramatic, spiritual encounter. This book offers the technique for working with the Spirit of God to present Christ alive!

PART ONE

Your Soul-Winning Plan

The HEART of this method is the PERSON of Jesus Christ Who is ALIVE this moment.

The REQUISITE of this method is your own personal EXPERIENCE with the living Christ.

The BASIS of this method is the WORK OF THE HOLY SPIRIT in making Christ real to a prospect.

The OBJECT of this method is to bring an individual FACE TO FACE with the Person of Jesus and urge him to RECEIVE the Lord into his heart.

Chapter One

Your
Soul-Winning Plan

---

*"Go therefore and make disciples of all the nations,
baptizing them in the name of the Father and the
Son and the Holy Spirit."* (Matt. 28:19 NAS)

Dr. Cortland Meyers one Sunday afternoon spoke to
a lad standing in the vestibule of Tremont Temple. He
said to the youth, "I hope you are a Christian." To Dr.
Meyers' amazement the young man replied,

"No, I'm not a Christian; but I know you and have
heard you preach for seven years."

Dr. Meyers then took him aside and in a few minutes
was able to do in a personal interview what seven years
of preaching had failed to do. It took **personal** attention
to reach this soul. How dramatically the effectiveness of
the personal ministry came to the good doctor. If salvation is finally a personal matter, then obviously the best
soul-winning is done at the personal level.

A person can sit in an evangelical church for years and ignore every invitation to go forward and receive Christ. That's because the invitation is directed to the audience IN GENERAL, and no one in particular. However, let one man confront another with the invitation to Christ and there is no escape. The prospect must say . . . "YES" . . . or "NO" . . . or "NOT NOW." **Regardless of his answer, he has made a decision.** That's why the Lord said "GO YE," making the Great Commission a **personal** matter (Matt. 28:19).

SALVATION IS IN A PERSON

The ONE TRUTH that must fill the heart and mind of the soul-winner is that Jesus Christ is **not a doctrine.** The Lord is a **living person** whom the grave could not hold, and at this very moment is alive and waiting to meet men in a personal encounter.

It is possible for a person to believe the Bible from cover to cover and be lost, for salvation is in the **PERSON** of Christ and not a book . . . not even the Bible. People must **meet** the Christ of the Bible and **receive Him** into their hearts or what they have is little different from the religions of the world. **This dramatic and personal event separates Christianity from all the religions.**

The worldly religions all have one thing in common. They ask people to accept doctrines, embrace systems and ways of life. Essentially they want men to **BELIEVE SOMETHING**; whereas the Word of God asks men to **RECEIVE SOMEONE!** There's a big difference between believing **something** and receiving **Someone!** One is little more than an opinion, while the other is an **experience.**

Amen!

15

It's not what a person **THINKS ABOUT** Christ that brings salvation, but what he **DOES WITH HIM.** The Bible says the "demons also believe and tremble" (James 2:19) . . . and the demons are definitely not saved. No matter what a person believes ABOUT Jesus, that will not get him to heaven. If life is in Jesus—and He said it was—then the only way to receive that life is to RE-CEIVE CHRIST (John 14:6). There is no way to separate the life of Christ from Him and receive it independently of Him. The hard fact is—one must H-A-V-E Christ in order to be saved. Note how forcefully the apostle John sets forth this truth:

"And this is that testimony—that evidence: God gave us eternal life and this life is in His Son. He who possesses the Son has that life and he who does not possess the Son of God does not have that life." (I John 5:11,12 Amplified New Testament)

Nothing could be plainer! If eternal life is **IN CHRIST,** then one must have Christ if he is to have eternal life. As far as John was concerned, the world was divided into two camps: the HAVES and the HAVE NOTS. Just as one must have a million dollars to be a millionaire, so must one **HAVE CHRIST** to be a Christian.

SOUL-WINNING, THEN, IS INTRODUCING PEOPLE TO JESUS *(Being Andrews)*

If salvation is in Christ, then no one can be saved apart from a **personal encounter** with Jesus. People must first MEET Christ in order to receive Him. That's what this book is all about. God has ordained that we who already know the Lord should be the ones to introduce Him to those who do NOT know Him. After all, He's not a substance that you take like medicine to get rid of sin.

He's a person with feelings, the same as anyone else. And He should be introduced to others as a **living** Person. What you are learning here is a plan for presenting Christ in such a way that people **MEET** Him in a dramatic, personal encounter. That's why this plan is called . . . THE ENCOUNTER-METHOD.

But you ask, "How can you introduce people to Someone they can't see? What kind of an introduction is that?" I know you're thinking about those who hold seances to make contact with spirit-beings, but we don't have to do that. Because of the work of the Holy Spirit, Whose task it is to make Christ real, we can introduce people to Jesus, the same as we would any other person.

Introducing Christ to a person is the same as any other introduction.

Illus: Today we say, "John, I'd like to have you meet Bill." The soul-winner goes beyond this of course, and says in effect, **"I'd like you to meet Jesus Christ** who died for you and now is eager to help you get ready for a wonderful life with Him in heaven."

There is no hand extended and neither is there a voice that answers when we speak to the Lord, for He does not operate in a physical body today. If He did, no one could receive Him. He must come to men as the omnipresent Spirit in order for them to receive Him **literally.** Also, this is the only way that **all of us** could have Him completely to ourselves. This naturally makes the introduction seem more difficult, but **we have help.**

HOW CAN JESUS INDWELL ALL CHRISTIANS AT THE SAME TIME?

When we say that a person literally comes into mens' hearts and lives, questions automatically present themselves. How can He, who is but one person, be in all of our hearts at the same time?

We are in a much better position to understand the presence of Jesus in our lives than were the disciples. The reason is because we have television. Does this surprise you? It is one of the best aids to understanding this mystery. Television, itself, is something of a miracle. Certainly it would appear miraculous to Peter and John—every bit as much as did Jesus' walking on the water. When we understand something of this modern miracle, we are in a position to comprehend the mystery of Christ's indwelling.

What we say concerning television, please remember, is simply by way of illustration. The analogy will not carry all the way.

In an oversimplified explanation of television operation, we find a scene takes place in a studio. By means of a transmitter it is sent out over television waves to the surrounding area. Anyone with a television receiver is able to pick up those waves and have a reproduced image on his own T.V. screen. The very scene of the studio is now transferred to his home. Not only is the scene reproduced in just one home, but in as many as **will receive** it. There is **no limit** to the number of sets that can receive the image from the studio; in fact, **"whosoever will"** may turn his set to the channel and receive what is offered.

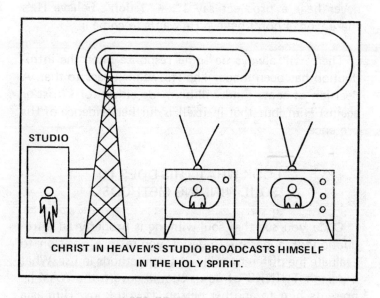

CHRIST IN HEAVEN'S STUDIO BROADCASTS HIMSELF IN THE HOLY SPIRIT.

If men can reproduce a scene, which takes place in a distant studio, in a multitude of homes, surely Jesus can reproduce His presence in as many lives as will receive

Him. In a peculiar sense the Holy Spirit may be likened to the transmitting waves so that the image that is formed in us is Jesus. We become receiving sets for the divine Transmitter. In this way we receive the Lord completely, and there is **no limit** to the number who are invited to do so. God would have every man tune himself to station J-E-S-U-S.

No amount of eloquence, dramatic technique or psychology can make Christ real to anyone. The **Holy Spirit** alone can do this and the worker must be content with his role as an introducer and leave this part to the Spirit of God. He will not fail. The Holy Spirit bears witness to the prospect's heart that Jesus is present and the successful soul-winner quickly learns this. Proof of this is demonstrated in every soul-winning interview, for you never hear a prospect say . . . "I don't believe He's there," or "I don't believe He wants to come in."

There will always be some response once the introduction has been made. The Holy Spirit sees to that. A **decision** of some kind will be made either for Christ or against Him, but that in itself is further evidence of His presence.

LOOK WHAT THIS DOES TO SOUL-WINNING METHODS

Once you see that soul-winning is properly an introduction of a person to Jesus, you're in a position to evaluate the different soul-winning methods in use. What a person THINKS of Jesus should govern the WAY he presents him to another person. If you know Him as a Person Who is gentle and kind, patient and loving, unselfish and sensitive to the needs of sinners, there are some methods you will NOT use.

You would not, for example, kneel beside a person at an altar and shout in his ear, "Have you got it yet?" Neither would you slap him on the back, insisting that he "pray through" to salvation. That is no way to introduce someone as nice as Jesus. You wouldn't introduce your mother that way. Neither should Jesus be subjected to such crude treatment. Such antics reveal a total ignorance of what the salvation encounter is all about.

● When I was in seminary, evangelism courses consisted mostly of Scripture memorization, with certain verses calculated to answer different objections that might be raised by a prospect. It was a sort of CATALOGUE METHOD where you expected to engage a prospect in some kind of a debate, hoping to win him over by answering his arguments with Bible verses.

Until the Lord gave me the plan you are about to learn, I went out on soul-winning forays armed with "9000 verses for 9000 situations." Needless to say, I didn't win many to Jesus that way. Everytime I answered one objection, the devil saw to it that the prospect had another. I spent all my time debating, never getting around to the actual introduction. Quite often, the interview would end in a dispute, a far cry from the sweet atmosphere of a pleasant introduction.

Finally it dawned on me, that if I were able to answer every single objection a prospect might raise, I would still have to introduce him to Jesus or he wouldn't be saved. That's when the Holy Spirit said to me . . . "Why don't you start with an introduction to Jesus?" I immediately abandoned the CATALOGUE METHOD and began developing (with His help) this introduction technique. It seemed logical. If men need to meet Jesus in order to be saved, why not use the time and skill to present Him ALIVE . . . **and let the Holy Spirit do the convincing.**

Note: If it is true that a person must open the door of his heart to Christ in order to be saved, then that is the place to begin. I have satisfied myself again and again that this concept is more honoring to the Holy Spirit and makes soul-winning easier and simpler. Therefore the method that is presented here is an **introduction.** Minimum time is spent on the matter of sin so that the positive truth of **receiving** Christ can be emphasized.

YOU NEED A PLAN

Have you ever had the agonizing experience of being with unsaved people and said to yourself, **"I know I should speak out for Jesus, but how can I get started?** How will I bring up the subject now?"

And then what happened? In all probability, time and the opportunity passed and you said nothing. Later you asked yourself another question, **"Why didn't I speak for the Lord?"** The answer is not hard. **You had no plan.** It is agonizing to be the servant of the Lord in a place of witness and not know what to say. But this happens every time a Christian does not have a plan and is not trained in its use. This is why **95% of all Christians have never led a soul to Christ.**

But suppose you do work up enough courage to speak for the Lord. What happens then? Usually the emotional content of the scene is such that your reason is overwhelmed and you cannot do a good job. Later, of course, you can think of a thousand things you should have said. But when you needed them, they didn't come.

22

This story is repeated wherever there is a Christian without a plan.

Every successful operation needs a plan and soul-winning is no exception. One does not dare build a house without building-plans; the walls might not meet. Why, even a trip to the market requires a planned list to insure that items are not forgotten. And God, too, has a plan for everything He does. Of all the Christian specialties this one certainly requires a plan. How brazen to assume that when God needs a plan for bringing men to Himself, we don't!

Every successful operation needs a plan and soul-winning is no exception. One does not dare build a house without plans, and God too, has a plan for bringing men to Himself.

Illus: A plan is to the soul-winner what a freeway is to a metropolitan highway system. A driver can be in a maze of suburban roads, yet knows if he can once get on the freeway, he'll be to the heart of town in the space of minutes. A smooth soul-winning plan gives the Christian worker the same facility. If he can ask his first approach question, he knows he is on the "freeway." In minutes his prospect will be face to face with the Lord. It is a plan that makes soul-winning easy.

If you have not yet weighed the advantages of using a soul-winning plan, here are some features you ought to consider:

1. It gives you a tremendous confidence that in turn produces boldness.

2. You have the advantage of knowing what reactions and responses to expect from your prospects.

3. **Your mind is relieved** of the stress of planning moves, leaving you free to concentrate on your subject and the Lord's presence.

4. You can **control** the conversation.

5. It makes you **stay on the target** and work systematically toward your subject's salvation.

6. It leaves you free to analyze the prospect's answers and responses and measure his understanding. You are not desperately wondering what next to say. You are able to **RELAX** in the Spirit.

7. You do not need a lot of Scripture verses or extra helps for the job.

8. You can bring your man to a decision faster.

9. You do not become confused.

10. Your prospect develops confidence in you, because you display confidence.

11. You do not torture yourself with, "How will I bring up the matter of Christ and salvation?" Memorized approach questions make it simple.

12. You will **always be ready** when the Holy Spirit gives you an opportunity.

YOU ARE IN COMMAND

Most of us have been on the receiving end of a salesman's "pitch" as it is called and have watched him fill out his contract even before we had indicated our willingness to buy. Shortly we were handed a pen and the contract and urged, "Just sign on that line there, please," or, "Would you approve this, right here?" There was no idle discussion of the matter then, we had to decide. We either accepted or rejected, in a **clear decision.**

Most of us have been on the receiving end of a salesman's "pitch." We either accepted or rejected, in a **clear decision.** In much the same way the trained soul-winner can bring his prospect to a decision for Christ.

In much the same way the trained soul-winner can bring his prospect to a decision for Christ. There is no middle ground as the soul-winner moves with surety and deftness right up to the point of salvation. It is his **conversation control** that makes this possible. He knows exactly what he is going to say each step of the way. He can even anticipate his prospect's responses. He is able to keep the conversation focused on the main issue and prevent unrelated materials from being introduced.

The controlled conversation technique is something new in evangelism and represents a real break-through in soul-winning. Older methods, dealing with excuses, seek to convince a prospect of his needy condition and humble him. Such efforts usually require considerable Bible handling, take longer and are easily thwarted by questions and intrusions.

The new method ignores excuses and completely side-steps the explosive area of religious debate. Modern soul-winners have discovered that it is unnecessary to change a person's mind before introducing him to Jesus. If he can be made aware of Christ waiting at the door of his heart, his **responsibility becomes most clear.** This makes soul-winning a positive ministry requiring fewer skills. It is a new frontier which makes Christian obedience a lot of fun!

Chapter Two

The Tools You'll Need

"Surely in vain the net is spread in the sight of any bird." (Prov. 1:17 KJV)

YOUR PERSONAL TOOLS WHEN USING THE PLAN

1. A pocket-sized New Testament.

Some soul-winners like to carry a small New Testament. In fact they feel naked without it. If you choose to carry one, it ought not exceed the popular 4½" x 6½" which is easily concealed in a lady's purse or on the person. Solomon cautioned, "Surely in vain the net is spread in the sight of any bird" (Prov. 1:17); a choice bit of wisdom for the soul-winner. The sight of a Bible under one's arm, a testimony at other times, is a hindrance to the soul-winning mission. It can create barriers and apprehensions not easily overcome.

Put tabs on your Testament. Secure some tabs from the stationery store and put them on the pages with verses in your plan. With these you can swiftly turn to your references with a single motion of the hand. Sometimes a delay in seeking a verse allows Satan to get in a question that will throw you off the target. Your plan **and** the turning to the pages of the Testament should move with clock-like precision.

Underscore in red the verses of your plan. This will insure that the prospect will spot it the moment you open to the reference. Pages should be clear of notes and symbols for they seriously hinder one seeking to locate the verse you are quoting.

OR . . . BEGINNING TO LIVE.

After carrying a small New Testament for many

years, the Spirit of God led me to develop a unique tool that would not only serve as Testament, but could also be given to a new convert to help him with his first doubts. This dual-purpose tool is a 24-page booklet called, **BEGINNING TO LIVE.** It is easy to carry in your shirt pocket or purse, making you ever ready for soul-winning opportunities.

Used as a soul-winning tool. Since the Encounter-Method uses only four verses in dealing with a prospect, four pages from my pocket Testament are reproduced in this tool. When you open it, the verses leap out at you. The prospect senses he is looking at a Bible and the Holy Spirit's witness gives it the impact of a Testament. When you use it, the verses are all together and in order of use. You don't have to go leafing through pages to find your place.

sample pages from BEGINNING TO LIVE shown at half the original size

Used as a follow-up tool. After your prospect has made his decision for Jesus, have him enter his name and the date on the NEW BIRTH CERTIFICATE in the back. After you sign it yourself, GIVE HIM THE BOOKLET. It is his to keep. Soon after you leave him the devil is going to assail him with doubts. "You don't really think you're saved do you? All you did was bow your head and say a little prayer. You must be crazy to think that will keep anyone out of hell!"

What will your new convert do then? He won't know what to do unless you prepare him. He'll be helpless unless you equip him to meet those first attacks. All he has to do is take out this booklet you've given him and it will show him exactly what to do to reassure himself that he's safe in Christ. That's why it is so valuable. They are so inexpensive you can give them away freely, something you might not be able to do with your Testament.

During the Vietnamese War, military chaplains used these in the thousands, not only to help those Christians who wished to be soul-winners, but as protection for their new converts. I have had many former servicemen write to me praising God for getting this booklet into their hands. Some said this was all that kept them close to the Lord while they were overseas and away from Christian fellowship.

2. Blank cards.

Keep a blank 3" x 5" card in your Testament in a convenient place so that you can slip it out for the illustrations. You will want an extra one in your pocket to write down names and addresses for follow-up.

OR . . . $5.00/FREE GIFT CARD

You've heard the expression, "A picture is worth a thousand words." That principle is exploited in the Encounter-Method by means of this **$5.00/FREE GIFT CARD**. Carried inside your **BEGINNING TO LIVE** booklet, it is used to demonstrate 2 vital truths. When you are explaining to your prospect the difference between believing in Christ and receiving Him as Savior, the **FREE GIFT** side of the card allows him to grasp that truth in seconds. The **$5.00** side is used to illustrate taking Christ in order to have eternal life. These truths and how to use the card will be explained in Chapter Five.

both sides of $5.00/FREE GIFT CARD
shown at half the original size

HELPS TO LEAVE WITH THE NEW CONVERT

1. BEGINNING TO LIVE. It's amazing how many truly born-again Christians lack assurance of their salvation. The reason **BEGINNING TO LIVE** is such an excellent follow-up tool is that it shows the new convert the THREE CHANGES that take place in a person when he's saved. Discovering them in his own life is one of the most powerful ways of assuring himself that he's safe in Christ. Once he discovers them he can RELAX in the Lord. Since they're built-in, no one can tamper with them. Once a new Christian is equipped with this kind of assurance, the doubts that come after that are good. They serve to make him check up on his salvation, satisfying himself that he is safe in the Lord.

2. SALVATION CLEAR AND PLAIN. Here's another 24-page booklet that is wonderful for the new Christian. It shows him, from the Scriptures, how his new life is not based on feelings, but on the fact of what Christ has done for him. Page after page presents his salvation as a miracle of God, rather than anything he has done for himself. This tool is popular with many TV evangelists, who give them to all those saved through their telecasts.

3. LOVETT'S LIGHTS ON FIRST JOHN. The only book of the New Testament written exclusively for new converts is the Epistle of First John. John says, "These things have I written that ye may KNOW ye have eternal life!" He uses the word "KNOW" 28 times. I have taken his 105 verses and compressed them into a 24-page booklet, along with my "LIGHTS" on the believer's two natures and the difference between sin and guilt, to give the new convert a delightful first contact with Bible study. Also, it answers some of the questions that bother a new Christian.

Your tools will include your Testament, a **$5.00/FREE GIFT CARD, BEGINNING TO LIVE, LOVETT'S LIGHTS ON FIRST JOHN,** and **SALVATION CLEAR AND PLAIN.**

Chapter Three

Some Hints That Help

"For the word of God is living and active and sharper than any two-edged sword, and piercing as far as the division of soul and spirit, of both joints and marrow, and able to judge the thoughts and intentions of the heart." (Heb. 4:12 NAS)

STAY ON THE TARGET

Satan will try to get you off the track and one of his favorite methods is to have the prospect ask a question about which you know a great deal. Be ready for, "What does the Bible say about the end of the world?" or, "How about Russia and nuclear weapons?" Questions such as these may come right "out of the blue," so be prepared for them. Be willing to pass up the opportunity **to show off how much you know.** Think back; how many times has this satanic device been used to get you off the track? Embarrassing isn't it?

Keep in mind you are **INTRODUCING** a person. If you were introducing one of your friends to another, you would not stop in the middle of the introduction to discuss something about either one of them, would you? No. And you shouldn't do that when introducing someone to Jesus. So don't stop in the middle of your introduction to **TEACH A BIBLE LESSON.** You can be sure Satan will cause something to be said that will touch on one of your favorite topics. You must pass up the temptation to show off how much you know . . . and **stay on target.**

When it comes to showing off, you can see how some might have a tendency to quote a lot of Scripture verses. Because they're necessary? No . . . indeed not. Satan leads them into it because they're secretly proud of the fact that so much Scripture can roll from their lips. Don't fall for that one. If you wonder how anyone could get into trouble quoting the Word of God, remember Satan is a master at turning good things to evil, as well as making evil things look good. It is a wonderful thing to store God's Word in your heart, but don't let it all out during a soul-winning interview. You'll get ego satisfaction all right, but your prospect will be turned off. In soul-winning, the Word is NOT to be used as club, but as **BAIT.** Four verses is just the right amount of bait.

DISREGARD CRITICISMS OF THE BIBLE

Regardless of the charge a person makes against the Word—**IGNORE IT AS THOUGH IT HAD NOT BEEN UTTERED.** This will seem awkward at first. The Word of God is the "SWORD OF THE SPIRIT" and that makes it a weapon!

Don't defend the Word of God—use it!

Illus: A fire breaks out in your barbecue. You seize the fire extinguisher on the wall and aim it at the base of the fire. But you don't pull the trigger.

Instead you begin explaining to the fire that you are holding a cylinder containing fire-retardent chemicals under pressure; and all you have to do is lift the handle and squeeze the trigger and a cloud of chemical will come out and extinguish the fire.

You don't explain a fire extinguisher to a fire—**YOU USE IT!** And so it is with the Word of God. **You don't have to explain it or defend it.**

That's ridiculous, you say! And you're right. You don't explain a fire extinguisher—**YOU USE IT!** You don't defend it any more than you would defend a gun to an intruder breaking into your home. Weapons are not defended, **they're used.** And so it is with the Word of God. **You don't have to explain it or defend it.** Since it is "living and powerful," it will do its job on those who question its authenticity or power (Heb. 4:12). A living sword needs no defense.

Even if you were successful in convincing a prospect that the Bible is the Word of God (which only the Holy Spirit can do anyway), you'd still have to introduce him to Jesus when you got through. By then, your time could be gone and it would probably be too late. Satan would rub his hands in glee at having diverted you from your target. It is an obvious tactic.

Illus: The writer has often confronted lads on the street with the Word and listened to such retorts as, "I don't believe that Book," or, "How do you know that Book is true?" or, "Who wrote that Book anyhow?" Their protests were completely ignored and in minutes tears were streaming down their faces as they invited Jesus into their hearts.

Those who disclaim the Word of God **are really debating with the Holy Spirit, not with you.** He continually affirms the truth to their hearts **as you speak.** Do not be surprised that people make strong untrue statements as they resist His convicting power. They will be directed toward you, but they are debating with Him. Pay no attention; be not disturbed. They are calling God a liar, not you. The fact that men refuse to acknowledge the Bible **does not reduce its effectiveness.** It remains forever "sharper than any two-edged sword." It is the voice of God speaking to men's hearts whether they like it or not.

DISTINGUISH BETWEEN RESISTANCE
AND RESENTMENT

Until he is saved, everyone is **RESISTING** the gospel. The apostle Paul says all of us were "ENEMIES" before we came to Jesus (Rom. 5:10). So we know there is going to be **some** resistance in every soul-winning interview, even if it is very slight. A person not resisting the wooing of the Spirit, would have already been saved. My point: **resistance is part and parcel of the soul-winning business.** We can expect it, therefore we should be prepared for it.

Every salesman knows about resistance. He realizes he will make no sale until he overcomes it. The same is true of the soul-winner. He faces the same thing. Yet resistance **CAN** be overcome by gentle pressures if they are applied in a sweet and loving way. People generally respond positively to someone showing a genuine interest in them. In making use of THE ENCOUNTER-METHOD, you will be applying gentle pressure to help your prospect do what he knows he should do—receive Christ.

Now if in the process of taking your man through the steps, you notice he is beginning to **RESENT** your efforts—**STOP YOUR PLAN AT ONCE.** If you persist beyond that point, he will become **HOSTILE.** You don't want that. When you generate resentment in a prospect, those hostile feelings will not only be transferred to you, but to the **gospel** as well. That would make it hard for you or someone else to deal with him again in the future.

So while you will be using pressure to overcome resistance, **you will NOT PRESS to the point of generating resentment. Hostility is the key.** When you detect **ANY** hostility creeping into the interview, that's time to stop your plan and say something that will allay his hostility and allow your interview to end on a friendly note.

You could say to him,

"I appreciate your letting me talk with you like this. I know it is a personal matter and you were most kind to give me as much time as you have. You're a nice person and I wouldn't mind having you for a friend."

That wouldn't fit every situation, but it gives you an idea of what I mean by breaking off the plan and preserving the relationship. If your prospect remains sweet toward you, he will respect your message, even though he doesn't receive Christ at the time.

GET YOUR PROSPECT ALONE

Do not try to deal with more than one person at a time if you can avoid it. This is especially true when working with minors. They are never themselves when another is watching. They will laugh and giggle and your ministry is thwarted. Even if you are in a home where all seem to be in accord, deal with the mother or dad first. Go through the plan with either mate, but address yourself to just **one at a time.** Remember, soul-winning is a **personal** introduction to Jesus.

USE THE PERSON'S FIRST NAME

If you do not know the first name of the person with whom you are dealing, it would be proper to ask for it after you have worked the 3 approach questions and are starting into the plan (Chapter Five).

You have just said . . . **"God says that we're all sinners. And we know this to be true in our own experience, don't we? By the way, what is your first name?"**

He answers, "Ed."

"All right Ed, let me ask this: Have you ever told a lie in all your life?" And your technique goes on from there, using the prospect's first name where it seems appropriate.

When you call a person by his first name, he gets the feeling you care about him. It is more personal. He feels closer to you. It is as though a friend is helping him, rather than a stranger putting his finger on his sin. And as you move through the steps, that closeness he feels makes it easier for him to listen to you and respond to your comments. Finally, when it comes time to present Jesus at his heart's door, the invitation to Christ is more personal. This is what God wants, of course, a personal invitation extended a man (or woman) He loves.

WHEN THE INTERVIEW IS FORCED
TO END PREMATURELY

On occasion you will be dealing with a person, when pretty well into your plan he is suddenly called away, or someone shows up, forcing you to stop. Maybe it is a phone call or he just realizes he's late for an appointment. Whatever the reason—**DON'T LET IT BOTHER YOU.** There is a tendency to feel frustrated when such interruptions occur. But it will help you to remember the TIMING is in God's hands. There are NO ACCIDENTS in this business.

Let's suppose you're dealing with a man over the back fence or in a parking lot, and he is eagerly moving toward the decision point. Then his wife appears from nowhere. She grabs his arm saying, "Honey, there's something at the store I want you to see. It'll only take a minute." What do you do then? Get upset? Has Satan sent an emissary to keep your man from Christ? Indeed not. The Lord has perfect control over the situation. HE could have kept the wife away, had that been His will.

41

Again, you might be dealing with a mother and one of her children has to go to the restroom. Don't allow a speck of resentment to creep into your spirit. The Lord is on top of the situation. He knows what she needs and WHEN. For this reason, it is wise to carry on your person a copy of **YOUR BIGGEST DECISION**. This booklet contains your soul-winning plan reduced to writing, and presented in such a way that the prospect can LEAD HIMSELF TO THE LORD. To use it, all you have to do is say . . .

"I know you have to go, it's been nice chatting with you. You can take this with you, if you will. It will explain what I wanted to share with you."

When you are equipped with a copy of your soul-winning plan in print like this, you're ready not only for interruptions, but also for those times when you run across a receptive prospect, but it turns out to be a "hit and run" situation.

If you are a press supplies salesman, and your prospect has to go back to work, you can give him a copy of **YOUR BIG-GEST DECISION**.

This is often true in sales, gas stations, offices, restaurants and department stores, where clerks cannot take time from their jobs for a fully developed soul-winning encounter. It is very comforting to be able to put into their hands a booklet that will do the same job you can do—when the Holy Spirit wants to work that way. It sure takes the frustration out of your personal ministry.

Note: I was serious when I asked you not to be concerned, should an interruption occur, putting an end to your soul-winning interview. The temptation is to think Satan is at work, frustrating your plan. More often, it is the Lord who is doing this, for reasons known only to Himself. Sometimes the prospect is not ready to go any further. The Lord knows he needs more softening before he is ready to be confronted with Christ. Again, you may have given the prospect all he can handle for the moment and the Spirit, aware of this, does not want you to press the person any further. So let your mind go to the Lord whenever an interruption occurs and thank Him for being in complete control of the situation.

Chapter Four

The X-Ray Approach Technique

"A wise man knows in his heart the right time and method for action." (Eccles. 8:5 NEB)

There are three approach questions with real psychological force that follow in **succession.** Circumstances may indicate that the first and second of these could be omitted; a little experience will teach you when. The questions are designed so that the prospect's answers make no difference and you can move on to the succeeding question regardless of his response. They expose his spiritual condition like an X-ray machine.

❶ "ARE YOU INTERESTED IN SPIRITUAL THINGS?"

The psychological force of this question is found in the fact that few people are willing to confess no interest in spiritual things. Here is a question that can be asked almost any place. Notice how little offense it carries.

Illus: If you are wearing an unusual Christian pin or attractive neckchain or a slogan that provokes an inquiry, you might reply, **"O, that's a Christian symbol. By the way, are you interested in spiritual things?"**

Illus: Let's say you have a "CHRIST AT THE DOOR" picture on a wall or a Christian art object in your home. Your neighbor comes to borrow something or to visit. As she (he) is attracted to the painting or art object and comments, you have a natural opening. A spiritual climate exists at once, and there wouldn't be the slightest offense were you to ask . . . **"Are you interested in spiritual things?"**

45

Illus: If you are a graduate of our **Witnessing Correspondence Course,** you are already familiar with the POWER OF PROVOKERS. If you are wearing an **ASK ME** pin or a **BORN ONCE, DIE TWICE** pin, for example, and it should provoke an inquiry, you'd respond with the corresponding tract. Should the prospect read it in front of you with seeming interest, you'd know the Holy Spirit had sent along a candidate for the gospel. How natural it would be to ask him . . . **"Are you interested in spiritual things?"** Thus your witnessing action would have generated a soul-winning situation.

The answer often comes back, "Sure, I believe in God," or, "My uncle is a preacher, etc." Regardless of how the person answers . . . even if he should say . . . "Not much," you can move right on to the next question.

❷ "HAVE YOU EVER THOUGHT OF BECOMING A CHRISTIAN?"

This one carries a bit more weight. Your attitude and voice tone are important. Be sweet and unassuming or there could be offense. The implication will bring some reaction. Notice the question **assumes the individual to be unsaved.** He is now in the place of having to declare himself for Christ if he wants you to believe him a Christian. Isn't this what our attitude should be toward anyone unless we have evidence to the contrary? Is it not unfair to **assume** anyone's salvation?

> **CAUTION:** In using the Encounter-Method, you would **never say** to a prospect . . . "ARE YOU A CHRISTIAN?" Why? Most individuals will always say, "YES." They feel that if they're not born to a Jewish family, and do not practice the heathen rites of a pagan tribe, they're automatically Christians. "After all," they reason, "isn't this a Christian country? Aren't we all one nation under God?" To avoid that, you must word your questions so that the prospect is forced to come out and say, "Why I AM a Christian." That is not easy for a person who has not received Christ. Usually it is only the born-again believer who will do this. So, discipline yourself against asking . . . "Are you a Christian?" You'll thwart your plan if you do.

The usual reply to this question is, "No, not much," or, "I've thought about it," or, "I used to go to Sunday

47

school when I was a kid." If the person turns out to be a genuine Christian, he'll come out and say so. But that's not easy for the non-Christian to do when the Spirit is convicting him of the fact that he isn't saved. So you've gained some information about the prospect's relationship to Christ. Your X-ray approach is working. It doesn't matter how he replies, your next question is easily in order.

❸ "SUPPOSE SOMEONE WERE TO ASK YOU, 'WHAT IS A CHRISTIAN?' WHAT WOULD YOU SAY?"

This question carries the greatest amount of psychological power, yet the inquiry does not damage your relationship. You have worded it as though **someone else** were asking the question. The phrase, "Suppose someone (else) were to ask you," removes sharpness.

With this device you have transferred any stigma to a **hypothetical** third person. It has the effect of putting someone else "on the spot," not you. Be sweeter yet. Gently offer your words with mellowness. A twinkle in your eye and a warm smile on your lips will relieve any tensions that might arise at this point.

Illus: This question is adaptable to varying situations. If dealing with a store clerk, you could say, **"Suppose a customer were to ask . . . "**

Illus: If you were in a home you could address the mother, **"Suppose your child were to ask, 'Mommy, what is a Christian?' How would you answer her?"**

Note: It is best to have a fixed approach technique when you are first beginning. Experience will show you how to increase effectiveness by tailoring style to meet circumstances. In time you'll learn how to adapt your approach questions to the situation.

The response that generally comes is, "Well, it's someone who believes in God and does the best he can."

You will agree with this, **"That's true, a Christian DOES do that, or at least he tries to, but what IS a Christian?"**

Thinking harder now, the prospect will try, "Well, he goes to church and prays . . . and lives by the Golden Rule, etc."

Once more you agree, **"Yes, that's true. A Christian tries to DO all those things, but just what IS he? He is different from all others. He has something no one else has . . . can you think what that might be?"**

When this is done four or five times, the prospect is finally exhausted of answers. Regardless of what he says, you can always counter with, **"Yes, a Christian does that, but what is he?"** A perplexed look will come on his face as he pauses to give more thought to the matter. About now it will occur to him that since he does not know what a Christian is, he himself, must not be one. He will not say this, but he won't have to. You'll know.

Note: Occasionally someone may offer a valid answer, "A Christian is someone who has accepted Christ." He may be parroting something that he has heard, but this is easy to test.

Simply ask him, **"Have you done that?"**

"Yes," could be his reply.

49

Then check with, **"Tell me about it. I'm interested."** This question is consistent with the X-ray
approach for it continues to expose his condition. He will not have to say too much before
you can measure him spiritually.

Also: People may respond with, "A Christian is someone who believes in Christ." This can be handled
in exactly the same way. Merely ask the prospect
to tell you **when** he became a believer in Christ.
Most respondents have in mind that a Christian
is someone who believes **ABOUT** Christ, rather
than in Him. They have never met Him in a
personal encounter.

YOU WILL BE TEMPTED TO, BUT . . .

At no time during the approach questioning should
you respond to an answer, "No that's not what a Christian is. He is . . . " and then proceed to give the correct
definition. You will find that you have simply given a-
way information which the prospect will turn around
and give back to you. That would thwart your plan.
Wait, for when it comes time to reveal what a Christian
is, you will be using the Word.

As you come to the end of the questioning (it just
takes a minute or so) the subject may say:

"I don't know. What is a Christian? You tell me."

Sometimes there is a pause during which he says
nothing. It is apparent from the look on his face that he
is exhausted of answers and does not know what to say
next. At this point, he is usually quite ready to listen to
you. In fact, he has to be quiet, for one cannot tell
another something he does not know. **HE HAS NOW**

RUN DOWN. He will not be interrupting you to tell what **he** believes as you present the plan. He's run out of answers.

Here are the three approach questions again:

1. "ARE YOU INTERESTED IN SPIRITUAL THINGS?"

2. "HAVE YOU EVER THOUGHT OF BECOMING A CHRISTIAN?"

3. "SUPPOSE SOMEONE WERE TO ASK YOU, 'WHAT IS A CHRISTIAN?' WHAT WOULD YOU SAY?"

LOOK WHAT THE X-RAY APPROACH DOES!

1. You have emphasized the fact that a Christian **IS** something, rather than someone who **DOES** something. The average person feels a Christian is someone who **does** certain things (works), rather than **being** something himself.

2. With just a few remarks you gain tremendous **insight** into the prospect's understanding of spiritual things. You're not in the dark about his spiritual condition.

3. The subject has shown **himself** that he is not a Christian. The truth is acceptable when it comes from his own reasoning.

4. You have placed the prospect in the position of having to **tell you** what is in his heart, rather than listen to a worker's lecture. Most words spoken **to** people are lost.

5. Your prospect has been forced to **concentrate** on his own need. All men are more interested when talking about themselves.

6. And most important, your prospect is **exhausted**. This will keep him silent as you present your plan. Psychologists agree that it is best to let people "**run down**" before attempting a presentation.

Now you are ready to use the Word!

Chapter Five

Presenting Christ Alive!

---

*"For the wages of sin is death; but the gift of God is
eternal life through Jesus Christ our Lord."*
(Romans 6:23 KJV)

Your prospect has just said, "I don't know what a
Christian is—you tell me."

That's the moment you've been waiting for. Hold up
your right hand so that FOUR FINGERS are showing as
you say to him . . .

**"If it's all right with you, I'd like to read you four
verses of Scripture and explain them to you—then you'll
know what a Christian is. That would be okay, wouldn't
it?"** (Nod your head affirmatively.)

Note: Man is a suggestible being, so suggestible in fact,
that he will respond to leading questions at the
slightest prompting. A simple nod of your head
has the power to activate your request. He'll find
himself answering you automatically.

"...I'd like to read you four verses and explain..."

At the right moment your **BEGINNING TO LIVE** is quickly produced from its place of concealment.

The request sounds simple and harmless enough. Surely four verses wouldn't take too long. Your affirmative nod will prompt most people to say, "Go ahead," or, "Sure."

Your hand reaches to your shirt pocket. The movement is so natural your prospect doesn't notice it. You don't take your eyes from his face as you bring forth a copy of **BEGINNING TO LIVE**. As you are doing this, say to him . . . **"God says that we are ALL sinners, as we see here in His Word . . ."**

Hint: If you are using a tabbed New Testament, the tab will help you turn to Romans 3:23 without taking your eyes off your prospect. If you are using **BEGINNING TO LIVE** (which I prefer) you know it is page 4. You don't have to look down. There's no fumbling. You know right where the verse is.

Hint: Do not stand in front of your prospect, but to his side. That way the discussion is not between you and him; instead, he is confronted with the Word of God. This creates the impression that the confrontation is between Him and God and takes you out of the scene. As he fixes his eyes on the verse, your words will carry more intimacy as they are spoken closer to his ear. Let your finger point to the verse so as to direct his eyes to the right place.

Read the verse aloud to him . . .

 "FOR ALL HAVE SINNED AND COME SHORT OF THE GLORY OF GOD."

Turn to page 4 of **BEGINNING TO LIVE**.

Your verse held in front of the subject confronts him with God's Word.

"God says that we are all in the same boat, that we are all sinners. We know this is true, don't we? For instance, have you ever told a lie . . . in all of your life?"

"Sure, who hasn't?"

"We all have, haven't we? Well then, how many lies does it take to make a liar?"

Hint: At this point hold up one finger just below the line of vision, yet conspicuously enough to be seen. It is so strongly suggestive that the prospect will always answer, "Just one, I guess."

Then continue, "That's right, rob one bank and you're a bank robber; steal one car and you're a car thief; tell one lie and you're a liar."

One finger held below the line of vision automatically answers, "How many lies does it take to make a liar?"

"And besides this, if the Lord Jesus were standing here alongside you right now (point to the location) would you say you are as holy and true and HONEST as He?"

Note: The average person recoils at being compared personally with Christ. This technique is used with the Holy Spirit to achieve the conviction of sin. The prospect has just admitted that he is a liar. In no way could he see himself as honest and true as the Lord. You don't need a lot of words to bring the conviction as the prospect pictures himself standing next to the sinless Savior. The personal comparison does it.

"If Jesus were standing alongside. . ." Point to the place.

"No, of course not!"

"Why not?"

"Well, I'm just not."

"No, and that is what God has just said in His Word, we are sinners and we do come short of His glory."

Note: All that you're trying to show now is that the subject is a sinner. As soon as he senses this, move on.

Hint: If you are using a tabbed New Testament, let your finger feel for the next tab. Open to Romans 6:23. If you're using **BEGINNING TO LIVE,** the verse is right across the page (p. 5), and it has not moved out of the subject's sight. Your finger simply slides across the page to the next verse . . . and you keep right on talking:

"Here we are, sinners by our own admission. But now we see that our sin has earned something for us. Because we are sinners, God says that we have something coming." Point to the passage as you read aloud,

 "THE WAGES OF SIN IS DEATH, BUT THE GIFT OF GOD IS ETERNAL LIFE THROUGH JESUS CHRIST OUR LORD."

"Here God says that the wages for our sin is death. We have already acknowledged our sin, therefore we have death coming to us as the wages for our sin."

Note: If you find it necessary to comment on the word death, you can say, "Death is separation. Just as

59

physical death is the separation of the soul from the body, so is spiritual death the separation of the soul from God. God says our sin has brought about our separation from Him. And this separation is eternal."

Then go on, "In this country, if you work for a man and have wages coming, the law says those wages must be paid. Now God's law is far more exacting than man's law. And when He says that we have already earned the wages of sin, we can be sure those wages will come to us." Pause.

Then continue, "That means that either WE must receive those wages, or someone else must receive them for us. That's what Jesus did for us on the cross 2000 years ago. In our place He received the full wages of our sin. So that now God is no longer speaking of DEATH—but the OPPOSITE—LIFE, ETERNAL LIFE . . . and as a gift!"

Repeat the last part of the verse again . . . "BUT THE GIFT OF GOD IS ETERNAL LIFE THROUGH JESUS CHRIST OUR LORD."

"Here we see that God is talking about a gift—that He has a gift for us (pause). You can't earn a gift, can you? You don't pay anything for a gift, do you? (Shake your head negatively, he'll understand and you can proceed.)

"All anyone can do with a gift is accept it or reject it, take it or leave it. Here God tells us that the gift He has for us is ETERNAL LIFE. That means we don't get it by being good or bad, or going to church, or being baptized or anything else. We merely receive it as a FREE GIFT."

Note: You will observe that some things are repeated. There is some of this, but not an awful lot. Remember, you are looking into the face of your prospect . . . and you're reading him. Sometimes you sense by the Spirit that it is necessary to REPEAT so that you can get a better reading of your man. You need to feel your prospect understands what you're saying before you can move on.

"We've seen that God has a gift for us, and what is that gift?"

"Eternal life."

"And now we see WHERE it is. It's in a PERSON. God has a free gift for us; that gift is eternal life; but it is IN a Person. I'd like to demonstrate that for you with this card."

Note: Now you are ready to use your $5.00/FREE GIFT card for the first time. Even as you are saying the words . . . "I'd like to demonstrate that for you . . . ," slip the card out of your New Testament or the booklet (actually it is just a few pages away). Hold it up with the $5.00 side showing so that it will catch his eye.

"For the sake of the demonstration, let's pretend this card is a real five dollar bill and I want to give it to you as a gift. But first . . . I put it in this book . . . LIKE THIS . . . and then offer it to you . . . you'd take the book to get the five dollars, wouldn't you?"

Hint: As he watches you, slowly and deliberately place the $5.00 CARD side up in your New Testa-

"Let's imagine that this card is five dollars. . ."

"But I put it in this book. . ."

"And then offer it to you. . ."

"You'd take the book to get the five dollars."

ment or the booklet and close it. Put the card into the book at the same time you are saying the words . . . "LIKE THIS." Then offer him the book with the card protruding from one end. He may try to take hold of the card and pull it out of the book, so be prepared to withdraw it before he can do that. Actually, he doesn't have to take hold of your Testament or booklet to get the idea. All you're trying to show with the demonstration is that just as the $5.00 is contained in the booklet, so is the gift of eternal life **CONTAINED in Christ.** It's as though Jesus is the wrapping around the gift, and there's no way to get it without receiving Him.

"Just as you would take the book to get the five dollars, so must you also TAKE CHRIST to get the gift of eternal life. The gift is IN HIM, and we must RECEIVE Him if we're to have it. And that's exactly what God says right here . . .

Note: The **$5.00/FREE GIFT CARD** is tucked in your Testament or booklet so that just a small portion shows to allow you to use it again. Now turn to John 1:12. If you're using the booklet, with a single motion of your fingers flip to the next pages (6 and 7) showing the second set of verses in the plan. On the left will be John 1:12 (p. 6). Observe that only a portion of the verse is shown . . . just that part which makes it clear one must RECEIVE the Lord. The rest of the verse could be confusing to a prospect.

Read the verse aloud,

 "BUT AS MANY AS RECEIVED HIM, TO THEM GAVE HE POWER TO BECOME THE SONS OF GOD . . . "

"Here God says that we need to receive Christ in order to become His children. Today, many people in our churches believe a lot ABOUT Christ. They believe in His virgin birth, His life of miracles, His resurrection and ascension into heaven; but they, themselves, will never make heaven, because they haven't RECEIVED Him." (Pause while this last statement registers.)

"There's a big difference between BELIEVING and RECEIVING . . . and again, let me demonstrate with this card."

Note: This time, bring out the card and hold it in your hand with the **FREE GIFT** side showing. Hold it as though offering it to him, yet just out of reach.

Then say to him, "**Just for the purpose of the demonstration (Ed), let's say that I offer you this card as a free gift. You believe me, don't you?**" (Nod your head affirmatively.)

"Ye-h," he will reply cautiously.

Hint: If he seems fearful you can allay his concern with, "**This is just a demonstration. I want to illustrate the difference between believing and receiving.**" He will relax and go along with you.

Then you can ask, "**You believe me, but do you have it?**"

"No, not yet."

"Here I offer it to you as a free gift, you believe me— and yet you do not have it, do you?"

"No."

"All right, now reach out your hand and take it from me. (The prospect does this.) **Now you have it, don't you? You have received it—it's in your hand, you've got it and you know that you have it, don't you?"**

Note: He may NOD his head in answer rather than speak. The dramatic participation has brought home a terrific truth. The senses of sight and touch have both been involved in this lesson. The difference between believing **SOMETHING** and receiving **SOMEONE** has just hit him with awful impact. This is the truth that separates Christianity from the religions of the world. He won't be stunned, but he will be deeply impressed. Don't

"I offer you this card as a gift—you believe me, don't you?"

"All right, now reach out your hand and take it right out of my hand."

"As long as it was in my hand LIKE THIS. . ." With these words, retrieve the card.

be in any hurry. Let the impact register. Then as you speak next, reach forward with your hand and **RETRIEVE THE CARD** from his fingers. You do that simultaneously with the words . . . **"LIKE THIS."**

"As long as it was in my hand, **LIKE THIS** (now it is back in your hand and you hold it up where he can see it), **you could believe and believe and believe and still you wouldn't have it, would you?"**

"No."

Note: The reason this verse is used is because of the one word, **"receive."** This key word shows that God's gift must be **received.** There are a variety of meanings for the word believe today, none of which comes close to the New Testament idea of acting on God's offer through Christ. In speaking of one's salvation, it is better to use **"receive,"** for the meaning is unquestionable. Now you are ready to tell him **how** to receive Christ.

"Well, just as you took **the** card from my hand, so must you also take Christ (pause) . . . **AND HERE'S HOW YOU DO IT."**

Note: Even as you speak, be opening to Rev. 3:20. If you're using the booklet, your finger slides a-across the page to Rev. 3:20 (p. 7).

"Remember we have said that God offers us the free gift of eternal life. That the gift is in the Person of Jesus Christ—and in order to have the gift, we must **RECEIVE** Him. Now listen carefully, for this is THE LORD JESUS SPEAKING TO YOU!"

Note: Here are the words that must be spoken in the boldness and authority of the Great Commission. They communicate to the prospect that Jesus is speaking to his heart, and not you. They also prepare him for the words to follow. Be firm now, for you are approaching the point in soul-winning where many drop out of the race. As you tell your man that it is the Lord Jesus speaking, look him in the eye and unwaveringly read with the **authority that is given you by God.**

"Now listen carefully, for this is the Lord speaking. . ."

OBSERVE: Though God gives us authority to speak boldly in His name, we must not forget that Jesus is the real soul-winner. Our techniques, skill and psychology are worthless except as tools of the Holy Spirit. Our authority is unlimited as long as it is Christ working through us. Did He not counsel us, "Without me ye can do nothing" (John 15: 5)?

As your finger points to the verse, say out loud,

 "BEHOLD I STAND AT THE DOOR AND KNOCK: IF ANY MAN HEAR MY VOICE, AND OPEN THE DOOR, I–WILL–COME– IN . . . "

Note: If you are using a Testament, be sure to leave off the remaining part of the verse. If you don't, you might find yourself sidetracked, having to explain the oriental meaning of "sup with him." It is a glorious subject, having to do with life-time fellowship, but this is not the place to discuss it. If you are using the booklet, you'll notice it has already been left off. You are about to present Christ ALIVE . . . and you want his mind ready for the decision just ahead. Read the verse slowly emphasizing the BOLD portions . . .

"The Lord says, 'BEHOLD, I STAND AT THE DOOR'—That DOOR, Ed, is the door of your heart."

Hint: As you tell him the "door" is the door of his heart, reach with your finger and tap him firmly just above the heart. This "live action" contact shocks him out of any dreamy state of half-listening to your words. It suddenly hits the prospect, "Wow! Jesus is here standing at the door of my heart!" The Holy Spirit anoints that finger tap to make it the most dramatic event in the prospect's life. After all, it's no small thing to realize the One Who made you is standing at the door of your heart!

70

"That door is the door of your heart."

Hint: If the prospect is a woman, a male worker should delicately TOUCH HER FOREARM with one finger. Ordinarily a man should not touch a woman, but the Holy Spirit will bless this action. Physical contact is needed here, for it shifts the conversation from theory to reality. However, I will leave it for you to decide the appropriateness of the gesture. Situations can vary. The prospect is now ready for your next words.

"Notice the Lord says, 'IF ANY MAN HEAR MY VOICE AND OPEN THE DOOR' (pause). That means anyone, man, woman, or child. If anyone will open that door, He says, 'I WILL COME IN.' " Let your words soak in.

And then continue, "You have a free will, Ed. God gave you that free will. And He won't violate that free will in any way. He won't force you to open your heart to Him. Even though He's the Lord of glory, the maker of heaven and earth . . . and even made you and me . . . He won't kick that door down and force His way into your heart. With all of His power, He stands humbly at the door of your heart, as if He had no power at all. He wants you to invite Him in. He wants you to open the door to Him."

One wouldn't hesitate to say "COME IN" to a friend knocking at the door.

Now lower your voice, speaking intimately and softly as you give an illustration.

"**If I were a good friend of yours, Ed, and came over to your house and WANTED TO COME IN and knocked at the door,** (tap on your Bible or any object close by) **what would you say?**"

"I'd say, 'Come in.' "

The response will be almost automatic. See the power of this technique? He is **using his lips** to express an invitation. This conditions him to voice the same words he will say to Jesus. You now have him ready for the big moment. **The most crucial part is next. Don't waver.** Don't let Satan lure you into backing away from the crisis, for nothing is accomplished unless you utter the next words . . .

"**All right, the Lord Jesus is waiting to come into your heart right now. WILL YOU OPEN THE DOOR? WILL YOU LET HIM COME IN?**" (Those might be the hardest words for you to say, but don't come this far and then fail. Say them . . . the Holy Spirit will back you to the limit.)

Note: **One of 3 things will now happen.** The prospect will say, "Yes, sure," or, "No, I can't," or he will say nothing. If he responds, "Yes," then the task is simple. The prayer of introduction is all that is needed. If he says, "No," he has already made a decision, but it needs to be clear to him. If he says nothing then press for a decision.

WHEN HE SAYS, "YES."

"All right then, would you bow your head with me

73

and I'll introduce you to the Lord." (You bow first and he will follow your example.)

"Dear Lord, thank You for being so gentle and waiting so patiently for us to open our hearts. You make it so easy. I know that You are anxious to meet Ed . . . and become his Savior. He is waiting to talk with You, Lord, and ask You into his heart. Here he is now."

Still bowed, whisper softly to your friend, "**Could you tell the Lord in your own words that you want Him as your Savior and ask Him to come into your heart? Could you do that? He is waiting . . .**" (Pause a few seconds to give him a chance to speak.)

Note: Sometimes it is easy for the person to speak to the Lord. At other times a prospect may find it hard to begin. "I . . . I . . . don't know . . . , " will indicate he needs a little help.

Say to him, "**I'll help you. Just follow me, if you will, out loud.**" Then in short broken phrases lead him something like this:

"Dear Lord Jesus—I know that I am a sinner—I want You as my personal Savior—I here and now open my heart to You—I invite You to come in—Amen!"

WHEN HE SAYS, "NO."

"You feel you can't do it right now, hummh? Well, I'm glad you're honest about it. It would be awful for you to pray with me and ask Christ to come into your heart and not mean it. It's better this way, but we do want to make sure of where we stand." (Pause.)

74

"Now let's be clear about this . . . I didn't ask to come into your heart, did I?"

"No."

"Then you're not rejecting ME, are you?"

"No."

"You're rejecting the One Who died for you, right?"

"Well, I'm not sure I want to put it like that."

"Even if it's only for the next five minutes, you are not about to ask Jesus into your heart, isn't that right?"

"Yes, that's true."

Note: Don't let this development discourage you. You have **NOT FAILED.** Your prospect **HAS MADE** a decision. The decision to reject Jesus and go to hell is every bit as big as the one to accept Him and go to heaven. What you have done has cleared the air. No longer can your man feel comfortable in "no-man's-land." He now knows where he stands. He is a rejector and knows it. All that is required of us as soul-winners is to be faithful in presenting the Lord. What people DO WITH HIM is their own business. We are 100% successful whether they make their decision FOR or AGAINST the Lord. A "NO" decision is just as valid in the sight of God as a "YES" decision. So don't feel you have failed, when you get a "NO." You have been very successful.

Hint: Even though your prospect has said, "NO," it may only be for a time. Depending on your skill and personality strength, you may be able to USE his "NO" decision in the power of the Holy Spirit. I can't take time to discuss it here, but you'll find the technique for using the prospect's rejection as a soul-winning device in my book **WHAT TO DO WHEN YOUR FRIENDS REJECT CHRIST.** Equip yourself with that KNOW-HOW and you'll be a "two-gun" soul-winner, able to handle people no matter which way they decide for Jesus. While your man has said, "NO," for the moment, the Lord still loves him and the Holy Spirit will continue to work with him. Knowing that, you could end the interview like this:

"Actually (Ed), you really don't need me or anyone else around when it comes time for you to receive Christ. This is something that is between you and Him. Why, even tonight as you lie on your pillow, you might want to talk to Him about this. All you would have to do is to ask Him to come into your heart and that you will trust Him as your Savior. It's that simple. He will do it too, AND IN THAT SAME INSTANT YOU WILL BE SAVED."

WHEN HE SAYS NOTHING

The person is silent because a terrible struggle is going on inside him. You give him just a few seconds to respond if he will and then you **must** act. Waiting too long is risky. Satan is very busy. This is the critical point. A question raised at this moment could divert your prospect from the decision. Be bold and keep your heart on Christ. Pray within yourself and you will sense the Holy Spirit's timing in **pressing for the decision.**

With the wisdom of a serpent and the harmlessness of a dove you can assist the person in his decision. You cannot **make** the decision for him, but you can bring him to a decision one way or the other. Every pressure Satan can bring is being exerted to keep him from opening the door. His heart is a battleground. The door is rusted shut and Satan does not want it opened. The Holy Spirit is seeking to open the door. Our skills and techniques become tools in His hands.

It is good though, to remind ourselves that no matter how much effort we expend or what techniques we use, it will be the **Holy Spirit** Who is dealing with the man's heart. Our efforts merely serve to reduce his **fleshly** resistance, while the Spirit imparts the grace to open the door. We have no part in that. We are simply introducers. Inasmuch as working with the Holy Spirit to open that door requires special skill, I am devoting a chapter to pressing for the decision.

Chapter Six

How To Press For The Decision

"Behold, I stand at the door, and knock: if any man hear my voice, and open the door, I will come in. . ."
(Rev. 3:20 KJV)

You have just said to your prospect . . . **"Jesus is waiting to come into your heart. Will you open the door? Will you let Him come in?"** He makes no reply. Great forces are at work inside him. His soul is a battle-field. The Holy Spirit and Satan want his decision. You wish you could jump into his heart and help him, but you can't. So you do the one thing you can do . . . press him to make a decision . . . **one way or the other.**

> **CAUTION:** You can't leave him in "no-man's-land." The longer you wait, Satan's advantage increases. So silently start your countdown. . .5-4-3-2-1. That's it. You wait no longer. Lay your hand on his shoulder (or arm if a man is dealing with a wo-man) . . . and with a semi-commanding voice say . . .

"Bow your head with me."

Note: **Do not look at him when you say this.** He won't act if you do. Instead, bow your head first. The sight of your bowed head, the authority in your voice, the touch of your hand on his shoulder and the witness of the Spirit combine to exert terrific pressure. Out of the corner of your eye you will see him look at you with wonder. Then, as his resistance crumbles, his head will come down in jerks. When your hand feels the relaxation of his shoulder, you'll know his heart has yielded.

Note: If your man is going to say, "NO," he has to do it now. You've brought him to the place of decision under terrific psychological pressure. If he can't bring himself to receive Christ, he'll say to you . . . "I can't do it." Then deal with him as you would the person who says, "NO."

He bows his head. You lead him:

"Follow me, if you will, and we'll pray together. 'Dear Lord Jesus—I confess that I am a sinner—and I here and now open the door of my heart—I invite you to come in—I now put my trust in you—as my personal Savior. Amen.' "

Hint: Occasionally you will take a person all the way through the plan and when it is time for him to invite Jesus into his heart, he will reply, "I've already done that." Perhaps he has. If so, then God has used you to strengthen one who was so weak he could neither identify nor speak of his own salvation. There are many like that, even though they have been saved, perhaps, for years.

79

Pause only briefly after you give the invitation. Then if the subject hesitates to answer, urge him to "bow your head with me."

This is powerful technique in LEADING a person to a decision.

AFTER THE PRAYER OF INVITATION, LOOK THE SUBJECT SQUARELY IN THE EYE AND ASK:

"Did you mean it when you asked the Lord Jesus to come into your heart?"

"Of course. I wouldn't have said it unless I meant it," most will answer.

"All right then, as best you're able, you have opened the door, haven't you?"

"Yes."

"And what did the Lord say He'd do if you'd open the door?"

"He said He'd come in!"

"Is He a liar?"

"No. He's no liar."

"Well then, if you have opened your heart to Him and He said He'd come in and He's not a liar, where is He?"

"He's in my heart."

"Yes. And that's how you know that you are saved. You see, it's not what you feel at this moment that is important. You may have icicles of emotion traveling up and down your spine, but the reason that you know you're saved is because you have done what God asked you to do and He cannot lie." (Pause for just a moment while the subject tries to appreciate the greatness of his experience—then make the test.)

"Now I'll ask you to do something on your own. Would you bow your head once again and this time say to the Lord, 'Thank you Lord, for the gift of eternal life'—just that much? Would you do that?"

"Thank you Lord for the gift of eternal life."

Note: Experience has shown this to be a wonderful test. The Holy Spirit will apparently not allow a person to pray this "thank-you" prayer unless he has actually received the gift. It is only courtesy to say thank you for a gift. Once in a while someone will not want to pray this prayer. Though it is rare, be prepared for it. Usually it is because the subject has gone through the plan just to get rid of you or he has made his decision in his HEAD, rather than his HEART. If you discern that he has failed to understand the message then take him through the steps once again. If he seemingly understands, but cannot pray, it would be wise to probe with, **"You didn't really mean it, did you?"** He will probably say, "No." You can continue with the dialogue for the "NO" decision in Chapter Five.

SOUND LIKE A LOT OF PRESSURE?

You might be sharing this approach with another Christian and have him protest that it sounds like a high pressure tactic. He would be right. It DOES use pressure. And any salesman reading this book would recognize instantly that it makes good use of pressure at the close. That's where all salesmen use pressure if they want to survive. You'll never see a successful salesman who doesn't know how to use pressure at the right time. In our case, we're using it not to sell, **but to bring them the greatest gift of all—eternal life.**

To object to this approach on the grounds that it uses pressure, reveals a lack of knowledge in two vital areas: **human nature and how the Holy Spirit works to overcome it.** In the first place, **people RESIST CHANGE.** We are all creatures of habit. We resent anything that comes along to move us out of our ruts. Why, we even have an expression that epitomizes this weakness . . . "DON'T ROCK THE BOAT!" By that we mean leave things as they are . . . don't make waves.

To get people to change, God has to use **PRESSURE.** He even uses tragedies to BLAST us out of our ruts. That's how reluctant we are to act even when we know it is good for us. And when it comes to getting people to accept God's invitation in Christ, the Spirit Himself is ever having to use pressure. You've heard people testify of being **COMPELLED** to go forward in an evangelistic meeting. "A hand seized me and literally dragged me down the aisle!" That's pressure. But sometimes God uses an auto accident, an illness such as cancer or the death of a child to get people to consider their need of His mercy. Now that's rough.

Consider the apostle Paul. You know what God did to turn him around, don't you? He knocked him out of the saddle on the Damascus Road and struck him blind for three days. That's plenty of pressure . . . far more than you'll be using in this plan. When you come right down to it, the ENCOUNTER-METHOD is one of God's tenderest ways of dealing with people. When He sends one man to another with a PERSONAL INVITATION to eternal life . . . that's **POLITE.** When that man puts his hand on the prospect's shoulder and says to him . . . **"I'll help you, bow your head with me,"** . . . that's **LOVE.**

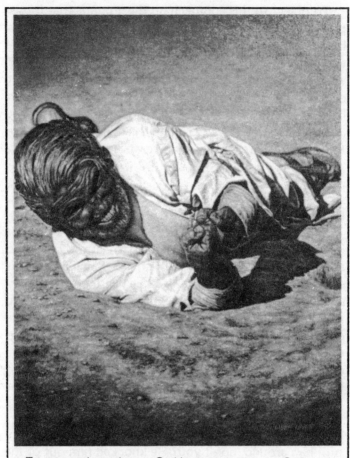

To get people to change, God has to use pressure. God used it to turn the apostle Paul around. He knocked him out of the saddle on the Damascus Road and struck him blind for three days. This is far more pressure than you'll be using in this plan. The Encounter-Method is one of God's tenderest ways of dealing with people.

I submit that while this method makes use of psychological pressure, it is administered gently and lovingly. If people resist this **gentle approach** God has **other** ways of reaching them . . . and they won't like that pressure. When your critic understands that, you should get no more protest.

YOUR COUNSEL TO THE NEW CHRISTIAN

As you behold your newly won babe, you will feel compassion as you think how important it is for him to be cared for and trained. Somehow he must be encouraged to take his place in the company of the redeemed and receive the encouragement that only a local church can provide. There is a remarkable sense in which the church of Christ is one large family and speaking in terms of the family relationship will provide him with his first counsel.

Say to him, "**Because you have received Christ into your heart, you are now a child of God. God is your Father! Remember the verse, 'To as many as received Him to them gave He power to become the SONS OF GOD!' This now, is true of you and you are therefore a member of God's family. You have many new brothers and sisters—in fact, you are my Christian brother now.**"

Continue, "I do not know what kind of a family you are from, but there is nothing more wonderful than a happy family where each enjoys and cares for the other. But what kind of family life would there be, do you suppose, if we never talked to our father, but selfishly ignored him all the time; where we treated him as though he did not exist and where he could say what he wanted, but we would never speak to him? That surely wouldn't produce a very happy home, would it?"

"No, I guess not."

"**Neither can we be truly happy in the family of God**

85

if we refuse to talk to our Heavenly Father. Our talking to God is PRAYER. Without that it would be an abnormal family."

"Now suppose that in our family, no matter how much our father wanted TO TALK TO US, we wouldn't listen to him. And no matter what he'd say, we would pay no attention. Would that make for a happy family?"

"No, it wouldn't," he will reply.

"Well, God our Father speaks to us through His Word, this Book—the Bible. When we read it, we are LISTENING TO HIM. As we talk to God through prayer and listen to Him as He speaks through His Word, there is a beautiful fellowship between us."

"But suppose in our family there were brothers and sisters. There could be no real happiness in a family where we would talk only to our father and ignore the other members, would there?"

"No."

"That's why church is important. We have brothers and sisters and they gather at least once a week to greet one another and tell of the thrilling things God has been doing in their lives. They talk things over as a Christian family and see how best they can care for one another. especially new Christians like yourself. Great joy comes to us as we learn how to live and work together as a family of Christians."

"The world doesn't like Christians too well. We have to stick together and look out for each other. You know, yourself, that you never hear any of these things on the job or on the street. Why, there the Lord's name is mentioned only in profanity."

"It is in the church that we learn the exciting things about the Lord Who has come into our hearts; and now you have the privilege of going to any church where Jesus Christ is truly worshipped as God and feeling a part of the family gathered there. As a matter of fact, I'd like to invite you to come with me to my church and let you meet some of your brothers and sisters. Going to church has nothing to do with your salvation. You already have that as a free gift, but you will find it necessary to enjoy the Christian life to the fullest."

Now you are ready to present the booklets. That's next.

Chapter Seven

Presenting The Booklets

---

*"I have written these things to you who do believe in
the Name of the Son of God so that you may
know that you already have life, yes eternal life!"*
(1 John 5:13 Lovett's Lights)

After you have led your prospect to Christ and con-
gratulated him on his entrance into the family of God,
you need to put something into his hands that will
serve as his first follow-up. Of course, you will get his
name and address. You need that for prayer, as well as
doing what you can to get him into a local church. Beyond that, he needs something that will help him with
doubts; reassure him that he's safe in Christ; and whet
his appetite for the Word of God.

Obviously, you are not going to be able to spend the
time with him it takes to do that. But neither do you
have to. The booklets that I mentioned earlier will do
this for you. So before he leaves your presence, you
make sure he is equipped with these three booklets:

1. BEGINNING TO LIVE
2. SALVATION CLEAR AND PLAIN
3. LOVETT'S LIGHTS ON FIRST JOHN

CONCERNING "BEGINNING TO LIVE"

Your prospect will be a little surprised when you say, "**Ed, I want to wish you a happy birthday!**" He'll chuckle, perhaps. But you're serious.

"**You see, this really IS your birthday. It's your SPIRITUAL birthday. And this is perhaps the most important day in your life. You're going to want to remember this date. And so it is important that we write it down.**" (Pause . . . as you open **BEGINNING TO LIVE** to the NEW BIRTH CERTIFICATE on page 21.) "**Now I'm going to enter the date right here on this line.**" (You do so.) "**And I'm going to ask you to put your name right here.**"

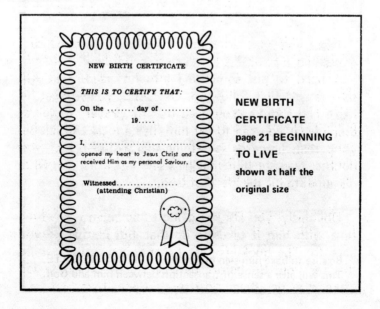

NEW BIRTH CERTIFICATE

THIS IS TO CERTIFY THAT:

On the .... day of ....
19.....

I, ...
opened my heart to Jesus Christ and
received Him as my personal Saviour.

Witnessed..................
(attending Christian)

NEW BIRTH
CERTIFICATE
page 21 BEGINNING
TO LIVE
shown at half the
original size

Shake his hand and congratulate him, "Happy birthday, Ed!" There is no way to conceal the joy that comes from introducing a soul to Christ.

Be sure to have him sign his NEW BIRTH CERTIFICATE. This will give a sense of transaction between him and God.

Hand him the booklet and the pen. Show him the place where his name goes. If he hesitates, say to him, **"This is your booklet. You are going to keep it. And you'll have the date recorded. I'll sign it for you after you enter your name."**

Note: Putting his name to the NEW BIRTH CERTIFICATE gives a sense of transaction between him and God. It's a feeling akin to closing the deal. While it has nothing to do with his salvation, it does reinforce the idea that he is now a child of God. Besides, it plays an important part when it comes time to reassure himself that he is really saved. Look at page 18 in the booklet and see how the certificate is used in dealing with doubts.

"Perhaps Ed, in a little while after I'm gone, a thought like this will occur to you: 'That was a strange experience. I meet a person who tells me of Christ. I bow my head and ask Him to come into my heart. Then he tells me that I am on my way to heaven. Surely, there must be more to it than that—just opening my heart to Jesus can't be enough to get me to heaven!' "

"When that happens, Ed, the best way to get rid of those doubts is to remember what took place here. Something happened, no one can change that. This little booklet reviews what we have said and it will help you to deal with any doubts that come along after some time has passed. Doubts will come and you need to know how to deal with them. Carry this booklet with you for a few weeks. Whenever doubts strike, take it out and read it."

ASSURANCE: One of the most fabulous things about this booklet is the assurance it brings the new believer. When doubts strike, **part of the reas-**

suring process is turning to the VERY SAME pages that were before him when he was being introduced to Jesus. As he looks at them, the Holy Spirit will cause him to RELIVE THE STEPS he took in opening his heart to Christ. When he can finally say . . . "I KNOW MY HEART IS OPEN TO JESUS NOW" . . . there is no way Satan can rob him of his new found joy. Besides, the booklet observes for him THREE DEFINITE CHANGES that are occurring in himself. When he discovers them in his life, he then has conclusive evidence that he is a born-again child of God.

CONCERNING "SALVATION CLEAR AND PLAIN"

This 24-page booklet is a bridge between BEGINNING TO LIVE and LOVETT'S LIGHTS ON FIRST JOHN. It offers a series of contrasts, explaining in sharp, concise statements what Christianity IS . . . and what it is NOT. For example, it will say on one page . . . NOT FEELING and on the other, BUT FACT. Again, other pages will contrast not by WATER, but by BLOOD; not a NEW LEAF, but a NEW LIFE; and so on. Under each of these contrasts he will see the Scripture verses that show what he has in Christ. Not many of them, but a few so that he gets a real witness that his salvation rests on the Word of God.

Present the booklet to him, saying . . . "Ed, you're going to want to know something about this new life you've received. And this booklet will teach you some of the first things a new Christian like yourself should know. You can read the whole thing in 10 or 15 minutes. I'd like you to read this tonight before you go to sleep along with your BEGINNING TO LIVE booklet."

CONCERNING "LOVETT'S LIGHTS ON FIRST JOHN"

"Ed, you may not realize it, but deep inside you is an appetite for the Bible. It's very faint, but it's there. I want to encourage you to begin studying the Bible. But don't do it because I want you to. There's another reason why you should dig into it and devour what it has to say. The New Testament is the Last Will & Testament of the Lord Jesus. When He died, His will became effective. It is in force right now. And you're mentioned in it. That's right. You have an inheritance that comes with being a child of God, but you'll have to read the New Testament to find out what it is." (You can see how that might whet his appetite some.)

"To help you get started I want to give you a copy

93

of one of the smaller books of the New Testament . . .
FIRST JOHN. It only has 24 pages and you can carry
it in your shirt pocket. Take it to work with you.
When you have a moment, take it out and read it. If you
like what you read, you're going to want to read more.
After that, I suggest that you begin a more serious Bible
study . . . beginning with the GOSPEL OF JOHN. It
was written by the same apostle who wrote this booklet."

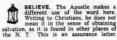

20. Now, if a man boasts of loving God, but keeps on hating his brother, he is a liar. He has seen his brother and has no love for him. What love could he possibly have for the God he has never seen? 21. No, the divine command makes the matter clear; he who loves God must also love his brother. It is impossible to love one and not the other.

"Can we love God apart from obeying Him?"

5 1. Everyone who believes that Jesus is the Christ (God incarnate), is born of God; and whoever loves the Father will also love His child. However, love for God is not possible apart from treasuring His commandments. 2. If we observe His commandments, we can be sure that we also love His children. Does that sound strange?

3. Obedience to His commandments is the way our love is expressed. Far from being a burden to us, His commandments are a delight, for they reveal His will. 4. Moreover, the person who is born of God triumphs over the world. Yet, this makes faith the real victor, since it is by faith that we are born of God?

5. The only one who can triumph over the world, therefore, is he who believes that Jesus is the Son of God.

BELIEVE. The Apostle makes a different use of the word here. Writing to Christians, he does not mean it in the sense of obtaining salvation, as it is found in other places of the N. T. This is an assurance letter.

20.

Therefore, "believe that Jesus is the Christ," is the result of salvation. Sit in a chair. Lift your feet from the floor. Say to a friend, "I believe this chair will hold me." Why? It already is. John finds that Jesus' indwelling produces this conviction. Such faith is the result of His work in us, not the cause of it. He is saying, only those who are born-again believe that Jesus is God. It is another assurance of salvation.

"What evidence is there for the truth of Christ?"

6. This is He Who came by water and blood - Jesus Christ. Not by water only, which stands for cleansing; but by water and blood, which represents the application of righteousness. 7. We have the Holy Spirit's witness for this and He is the Spirit of Truth. 8. So there are three who bear witness, the Spirit, the water and the blood. These three concur as one and they are one.

INTERNAL WITNESS. When a person receives heaven's witness within himself, it is unshakable. True, it is subjective and others can challenge it for that reason. But the witness is not for others. It is for the Christian himself. When truth rises within a man, he is freed from having to look to others or outside sources for confirmation. The water and the blood have stood for cleansing and applied righteousness from the first days of the Old Testament where they foretold Christ's work for man. One could not go far wrong in interpreting the water as the Word of God, the blood as the applied holiness of the new nature and the witness of the Holy Spirit as God's voice within our own souls.

21.

sample pages from LOVETT'S LIGHTS ON FIRST JOHN shown at half the original size

Note: FIRST JOHN was written for new Christians. And it is an ideal portion to place in the hands of your new babe. He'll thrill to the idea that he can KNOW that he HAS eternal life. After a week has gone by, you may wish to give your convert a copy of JOHN'S GOSPEL, and if you like the style of LOVETT'S LIGHTS, the gospel is available in that form too. Also, a week later, you may wish to place in his hands a copy of **BEGINNING TO PRAY.** It will show him how to develop a conversational type relationship with the Lord, learning to chat with Him about everything that occurs in his life. If you can bring your new convert to this point, you will have a very choice gift to lay at the feet of our Lord Jesus.

FINAL WORDS BEFORE YOU SEPARATE

Say to him, "Now Ed, if someone were to ask you, 'Are you a Christian,' what would you say?"

"I'd say, 'Yes, I am.' "

"But, suppose he says, 'How do you know you are a

Christian,' how would you answer him?" (The convert may pause. If he does, ask him:)

"What did you ask Jesus to do?"

"To come into my heart."

"Did He?"

"Yes, He did."

"That's how you know you are a Christian. You have asked the Lord to do something that He said He would do and He cannot lie!"

These parting words bring strength to the new Christian. The final emphasis helps to keep them in remembrance. So much has happened and has been said that he will be able to remember little of it. About all that he can be sure of is that he has made a decision for Christ. This is the point you seek to drive home.

Now you are ready for PART TWO which gives you the technique for learning the plan.

PART TWO

Using Your
Soul-Winning Plan

Chapter Eight

Learning The Plan

*"And He said to them, 'Go into all the world
and preach the gospel to all creation.' "*
(Mark 16:15 NAS)

By now I trust you are satisfied that the ENCOUNT-ER-METHOD of soul-winning is a most powerful technique for bringing people face to face with Jesus. Equipped with this kind of KNOW-HOW, a Christian can make himself available to the Holy Spirit and know for certain that he can win souls. Yet, is not the best plan in the world useless—until you know how to put it into action? Here then, are the steps for easing yourself into action . . . as a soul-winner . . . using the Encounter-Method.

1. READ THE DIALOGUE PORTION OF THE PLAN SEVERAL TIMES.

See if you can gain an overall FEEL for it without trying to fix any of it in your mind. Then write out on a card the **FOUR VERSES** as listed on pages 111 & 112. Between each verse write out the corresponding **TRANSITION LINES** which get you from verse to verse as listed on page 110.

Hint: A 3 x 5 inches **SOUL-WINNING LAB CARD** is available to you from **Personal Christianity** with the verses and transition lines already printed out so that you can hold the card in your hand and **practice the plan** without having to refer to the book. Naturally, you won't be able to do this at first, but with a bit of practice you will be able to go through all the steps, simply by using the card. The card not only makes for easier memorization, it also serves as a "bridge" in going from the book to being able to use the plan without any kind of an aid. It is especially helpful when practicing the technique with another Christian. Such a card is a MUST for actual laboratory classes held in churches and Bible schools.

2. MEMORIZE THE PRESENTATION

. . . so that you have it almost word perfect. To get the plan firmly fixed in your mind, it will help if you make use of my **SOUL-WINNING DEMONSTRATION CASSETTE.** On Side One I personally take a prospect through the presentation without interruption. Side Two contains a demonstration of the rejection technique. If you are a housewife, you can listen to it while ironing or working at the sink. A husband can listen to it in the car on his way to work. You don't have to concentrate as you listen. Yet, hearing it again and again actually sets the plan in your memory. You'll be amazed at how easily it comes to your lips after you have used this cassette for a time.

99

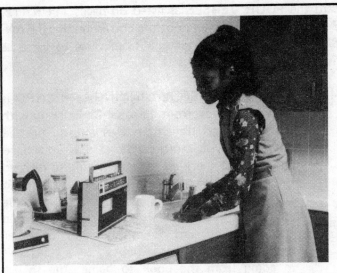

In order to get the plan firmly planted in your mind, a housewife might listen to the **SOUL-WINNING DEMO-NSTRATION CASSETTE** while at the sink. . .

or. . .a husband can listen to it in the car on the way to work.

Note: The best sales organizations require their sales people to learn the company presentation word for word. They even hold practice sessions at their sales meetings to make sure the sales force is using the plan as developed by the company. In this way, they know their salespeople are not fumbling for words, but able to focus on the prospect . . . watching to see that his mind is captured . . . right down to the close. We should not give the Lord any less. An essential part of easing yourself into action, is getting the plan down pat.

The best sales organizations hold practice sessions for their sales people to learn the company presentation word for word. That way they are able to focus on the prospect. . . right down to the close. The soul-winner should do the same—for the Lord!

3. PRACTICE WITH THE PLAN.

After you have learned the plan to the place where you can go through the steps using the 3 x 5 in. **LAB**

CARD alone, it is time to practice with someone else. If husband and wife are both saved, your mate could be an ideal person. Again, you may have a Christian friend who is closer to you in the things of the Lord, in which case this would be the one with whom you might practice. Of course if you are in a soul-winning class, this is automatically cared for.

Seat yourself beside your practice prospect so that you hold your Testament or **BEGINNING TO LIVE** booklet in front of him. Put the **LAB CARD** on your knee so that you can glance at it while you are making the presentation. Even though you have to stop and think . . . and perhaps feel awkward doing this . . . bear in mind it is just a practice session. You have to start some place. No matter how clumsy your first attempt seems, it will be twice as good the next time . . . and a lot better the third time.

Hint: Satan will naturally emphasize your initial clumsiness in an attempt to discourage you. Don't let him get away with it. Every new thing we try is awkward at first, and soul-winning is no exception. So don't give up because you feel a little foolish or have to make long pauses as you are thinking of what comes next. It will all smooth out in time. The Holy Spirit wants you to stick with it and He'll help you. If you stay with it, you'll be surprised at how quickly you'll master it.

Hint: In the early stages of working with your plan and learning how to handle your Testament or **BEGINNING TO LIVE** and **$5.00/FREE GIFT CARD**, make use of a full length mirror. Stand before the mirror, pretending an unsaved prospect is beside you. Watch yourself in the glass as you go through the steps. The purpose? To see yourself as your prospect sees you. Take note of your gestures, particularly how you move your hands and head. See if you're holding the booklet or Testament at the right level. Think about your personality gifts and how you make the most of them. Practice putting the card in the booklet or Testament. See how you look doing this. Do this several times and the Lord will show you how to put some polish on your work for Him.

In the early stages of learning how to handle your tools, stand before a full length mirror, pretending an unsaved prospect is beside you. See yourself as your prospect sees you.

• If you happen to be in a church currently teaching the Encounter-Method of soul-winning, join the class. A class is the best place to learn the plan, because the lab sessions give you a lot of actual practice with different partners. There is very little embarrassment, since all the students are in the same boat. Everyone is at the same learning level.

In a class you can watch the teacher demonstrate the plan . . . and then let your eyes follow along on the **LAB CARD.** You learn to associate the actions with the lines on the card. This in turn makes it easier for you when you begin practicing with another student. In other words, you move in stages . . . from the teacher . . . to the card . . . to an actual exercise. A lab class is the best place to learn the plan.

Note: If your church doesn't have such a class under way, you might be the one to suggest it. We have a teacher's guide that makes it easy for anyone desiring to teach this method in a classroom situation. If you are in Bible school or college, and learning the Encounter-Method as part of your evangelism training, you would be an ideal person to get such a class going in your local church. Not only would you give the Lord some soul-winners, but you would become extremely sharp in the skill simply through teaching it.

4. PRACTICE WITH THE PLAN UNTIL YOU CAN MAKE A SMOOTH PRESENTATION.

You need to know your plan perfectly and be able to use it without having to worry over what you are going to say next. This makes you FREE to watch for two things: **(1) the understanding of your prospect, and (2)**

the working of the Holy Spirit. If you are occupied with yourself, worried over what you are going to say next, your prospect's mind could wander and you'd never know it. You'd go right on without realizing you'd lost him. But if you know your plan thoroughly, you are FREE from such worry, able to read his face and measure his understanding. Only then do you know whether or not you have to slow down or go back and make a point more clear.

Note: What we're after is a SHIFT IN EMPHASIS from you to your prospect. When a man has to fumble for words and doesn't know what he is going to say next, he is so occupied with himself he is oblivious to what is happening in his prospect. Also, there are definite signs on the face of a prospect that indicate the working of the Holy Spirit. A look in the eye, a movement of the lips (especially around the corners of the mouth) can be read like words on a page. If you are free to watch for it, you can observe the Holy Spirit's ministry to your prospect. This is so helpful when it comes time to press for a decision. If you can't see what the Spirit of God is doing, there is no way to cooperate with Him. Hence my strong emphasis on knowing your plan so well that you can make a smooth presentation. And that takes practice.

5. WINNING YOUR FIRST SOUL.

Once you have learned your plan, you are ready to USE it. The name I give to this first effort is . . . **"coffee cup evangelism."** You'll see why shortly. I want you to consider this step as an actual assignment. Here's how it works:

Invite an unsaved friend or neighbor over for a cup of coffee or a snack. Explain to him (or her) that you are taking a course and one of your assignments is to practice on someone. Explain that it is practice only and that you appreciate his help. This serves to disarm your prospect. He won't find any threat in something that is for practice only . . . and particularly so, if you mention that you might be a little awkward and clumsy, because you are just learning. That will set him at ease.

"Coffee cup evangelism" is a great way to ease into the plan.

Then go through the steps, including the three approach questions. The X-Ray technique will tell you a lot about your prospect even before you begin your presentation. Finally you reach the place where Jesus is knocking at the door of his heart. You have lowered your voice and said to him . . .

"If I were a good friend of yours, Bill, and came over to your house and WANTED TO COME IN . . . and knocked at the door . . . (tap on the table) . . . what would you say?"

"I'd say, 'Come in.' "

At this point you shift your role. Instead of playing the part of a student learning the plan, you now assume the role of a soul-winner. You continue in this fashion . . .

"You know, Bill, it's true this is just a practice session. And I appreciate so much your willingness to help me. But you know, Jesus really is at the door of your heart. He's waiting to come in right now. Will you open the door? Will you let Him come in?"

● It is actually common to find the Holy Spirit has selected a person ready to receive the Lord. You will probably be amazed at how easily your prospect bows his head with you and asks Jesus into his heart. It would seem the Lord wants new soul-winners to have this kind of encouragement the first time out. It is almost as if He deliberately supplies a prepared prospect for the initial encounter.

Note: Your joy will be boundless at the winning of your first soul. You'll find yourself practically shouting praise to God. But make sure you're alone when you do this. Anyone seeing you so filled with the spirit of joy will think you're off your rocker. But don't let it go to your head. First thing you know, you'll find yourself **judging** those of your brethren who are sitting in the churches doing nothing for Jesus. Satan will plant this idea in your mind almost immediately, hoping to turn your new adventure in the Spirit into an evil thing. We're not called to judge our brothers, even Jesus doesn't do that . . . until the appointed day. If you feel sorry for them, the thing to do is to share your know-how with them.

6. ADAPT THE PLAN TO YOUR OWN PERSONALITY.

After you've won your first soul, you'll be on your way. From this point on, you no longer need to follow the plan precisely as I have given it to you. You can now change it to suit yourself. Feel free to drop parts of the dialogue, if you wish, and add lines of your own. If you wish to incorporate illustrations you feel are more appropriate, do so. **In time you will have your OWN plan, able to make a presentation that is perfect for you.** But to get you started, it is best to learn the plan exactly as I have laid it out for you.

The truth is, you will encounter situations where you do have to make changes anyway. It could be that you live or work in an environment where the approach questions should be modified to suit your situation. I'll show you what I mean by giving you . . .

an adaptation of the three approach questions.

Let's assume you work for a Christian organization. On a particular day you are near the receiving room door, when a delivery truck arrives. The driver hops out and unloads a big box on the floor. Before he returns to his truck, he hands you a clipboard and says . . . "Will you sign for this?"

As you are acknowledging the delivery, you ask him a question. . .

"Are there other Christian organizations on your route?"

"There are."

"Do any of the people you meet there ever talk to you about spiritual things?" You watch his reaction closely.

"Sure, once in a while." The tone of his voice and attitude tell you something.

"What if one of them were to ask you, 'What is a Christian,' what would you say?"

See—it's not hard to adapt the approach questions to a particular situation. It's even fun, once you get the idea. The Holy Spirit is ready to give this kind of wisdom if you ask Him for it.

LEARNING THE TRANSITION LINES

The steps I have laid out above show you how to go about learning the plan. You can see that I stress learning the plan so well that you can almost recite it verbatim. Now we're going to look at some things that will give you an even better grasp of the Encounter-Method. The best way to start making the plan a part of you is by memorizing the **transition lines**. There is an advantage in this. Should you inadvertently find yourself in a soul-winning situation before you have the plan down pat . . . and this could happen . . . you'll at least know how to move from verse to verse. A

109

smooth presentation depends on your ability to go easily and quickly to each of the four verses. Here are the **seven transition lines:**

1. **"If it is OK with you, I'd like to read you four verses of Scripture and explain them to you and then, etc."** (Leads into plan.)

2. **"God says that we are all sinners, for we read here . . . "** (Leads into Rom. 3:23.)

3. **"And because we are sinners (by our own admission) we see that our sin has earned something for us."** (Leads into Rom. 6:23.)

4. **"And because of what Christ has done for us, God speaks of something else. Here He is speaking of a gift."** (Leads into last portion of Rom. 6:23.)

5. **"And just as you would take the book to get the five dollars, so must you also receive Christ in order to have the gift of eternal life. And that's what God says here . . . "** (Leads into John 1:12.)

6. **"So must you also take Christ and here's how we do it. This is the Lord Jesus speaking to you . . . "** (Leads into Rev. 3:20.)

7. **"He is waiting to come into your heart right now. Will you open the door? Will you let Him come in?"**

Inasmuch as most Christians do not have any sort of a plan for soul-winning, the best way to acquire individual skill is to learn the plan that is presented here **first.** Then as one's personality strength dictates, branch out into his own variation of it. The basic idea will always remain, that is, that eternal life is in the **Person of Christ**, and to be saved, one must receive Christ in a personal experience.

TO BE SAVED, A PERSON TRAVELS FOUR DISTINCT STEPS:

1. He discovers that he is a sinner and his sin has separated him from God.

2. He hears that he need not be separated from God any longer for Christ has died for Him and now God offers him eternal life.

3. He discovers that he may receive the free gift by receiving Christ.

4. He is confronted with Christ at the door of his heart and asked to let Him in.

THE FOUR STEPS ARE TRAVELED BY MEANS OF FOUR VERSES

1. **Rom. 3:23**—"FOR ALL HAVE SINNED . . . " Teaching that **all men** are sinners.

2. **Rom. 6:23a**—"WAGES OF SIN IS DEATH." Teaching that sin earns the wages of **eternal separation** from God (death).

   Rom. 6:23b—"BUT THE GIFT OF GOD IS . . . " Teaching that God offers men the **free gift** of eternal life (union with God) and the gift is **IN** the Person of Jesus Christ.

3. **John 1:12**—"BUT AS MANY AS RECEIVED HIM . . . " Teaching that Christ must be **RECEIVED** to have the gift.

4. **Rev. 3:20**—"BEHOLD I STAND AT THE DOOR
. . . " Teaching that Christ is received by **inviting** Him
into one's heart.

DRAMATIC TECHNIQUE GIVES LIFE
TO THE VERSES

Rom. 3:23—Two questions make the verse very effective.

    a. **"Have you ever told a lie, in all of your life?"** The
       finger held just below the line of vision answers the
       question, **"How many lies does it take to make a
       liar?"**

    b. **"If the Lord Jesus were standing beside you right
       now . . . "** produces a surprising emotion. The,
       "Of course not," is followed by, **"Why not?"**

Rom. 6:23a—Illustrated by the national law guaranteeing
wages to a worker.

Rom. 6:23b—Pretending the card to be a $5.00 bill and
placing it in the Testament or booklet demonstrates the
truth that the gift is **IN** Christ.

John 1:12—The card (free gift side) dramatically teaches
the difference between believing and receiving. That lesson is taught to the prospect as a part of the plan.

Rev. 3:20—This verse uses the most of drama. Three
things make the experience real to the prospect.

    a. Tapping on his heart to indicate the door.

    b. Asking what he would say in answer to a knock at
       the door.

c. Your command for him to bow his head with you.

DRAMATIC TECHNIQUE GIVES POWER
TO YOUR PLAN

1. Your finger held just below the line of vision always provokes the desired response. As one need steal but one car to become a car thief and rob but one bank to become a bank robber, so does one lie make a liar. This points out the truth that the prospect is a liar and **has a need.**

2. By reaching and taking hold of the card he gets the sense of **appropriating** to himself that of which you speak. The sense of touch is employed.

3. You shock him out of any dreamy state of half-listening to your words as you tap on his heart. He suddenly realizes it is **his own heart.** Automatically it comes to him, "My heart."

4. Using his **lips** to say, "Come in" prepares him to say the same words to Jesus at the moment of invitation.

5. Your **hand** laid firmly on his shoulder at the instant of your command to bow, gives you an **authority** that is difficult to resist.

6. The sight of your bowed head brings the whole matter to its **climax.** He must do something then.

SOMETIMES THE SITUATION CALLS FOR
AN ABBREVIATED PLAN

If you are dealing with a prospect and the X-Ray technique reveals he has a background of Bible knowledge, it is not necessary to take him through the whole plan. Let's return to the scene with the truck driver making a delivery to your Christian organization and I'll show you what I mean.

You have just asked him to tell you what a Christian is . . . and his reply is not at all what you might have expected . . .

"I recently married a Catholic girl and I'm going to a class where we're learning all about this stuff. So I'd say a Christian is someone who believes that Christ is the Son of God . . . and that He died for our sins, and if we confess our sins, God forgives us."

● What does a response like that tell you? You don't have to go through the whole plan with him. Obviously he has enough knowledge to be saved. All that is necessary now is determining whether or not he has actually received Christ. Thus, you could make your adaptation something like this:

"In this class you go to, are they teaching you that it is necessary to receive Christ to be saved? That simply believing the things they're teaching about Him won't save anyone . . . that a person must actually DO SOMETHING about Christ?"

"What do you mean?" That would be the expected reply. Or, he could say, "No."

At that point you would quickly bring forth your Testament or **BEGINNING TO LIVE** booklet, opening it to John 1:12. (No Bible has been in sight to alarm him, so there's no barrier to overcome.) Say to him . . .

"God says, 'BUT AS MANY AS RECEIVED HIM,

114

TO THEM GAVE HE POWER TO BECOME THE SONS OF GOD.' Today, many believe all kinds of things ABOUT Christ. They believe in His virgin birth, His life of miracles . . . etc."

From this point on, you would take him through the rest of the plan.

Rule: When it is obvious your prospect has an understanding of sin and salvation, there is no need to go through the first two steps. Simply find a way to bring up the matter of RECEIVING Christ . . . and begin the plan at John 1:12. Once your man sees the difference between BELIEVING and RECEIVING, move quickly to the close. You may also run into a situation where all that is needed is the last step . . . Rev. 3:20. If for example, a friend of yours is dying and has simply been putting off his decision to receive the Lord, all you would need do is tell him Jesus is waiting to come into his heart at that moment and ask him, **"Will you open the door?"**

Now you're ready for the important part psychology plays in soul-winning. Next.

Chapter Nine

Psychology And
The Soul-Winner

---

*". . .solemnly testifying to both Jews and Greeks of
repentance toward God and faith in our Lord
Jesus Christ."* (Acts 20:21 NAS)

God has given us a superb tool in psychology. It plays
an important part in soul-winning today. In the past,
many were afraid of the term, thinking it was a science
opposed to the Word of God, but now they know this is
not so. Many of those same people are now excited over
the increased effectiveness this God-given help can bring
in Christian service. The soul-winner particularly enjoys
a wonderful advantage through the power of psychological insight.

One is not long involved in winning men to Jesus before he discovers, that from the very first mention of
spiritual things, there is a desperate attempt to set up a
smoke screen. There is obvious desperation on the part
of many to avoid the Person of Christ. They will say
almost anything to keep from being confronted with

their responsibility to God. How they sputter and squirm: "I have my own ideas on religion; I have a brother who is a missionary. I do the best I can and I believe that I will get by all right." Were it not so tragic, one could almost laugh at the obvious panic that sets in when it appears the Lord is about to become the center of the conversation.

• The popularity of religion in America today has produced this smoke screen. A religious wave is presently sweeping our land to the place where it is fashionable for radio announcers to conclude broadcasts with Bible verses, while others find it convenient to end their programs with, "God bless you" and other clichés. With people attending church in increasing numbers with the bulk of them unsaved, crowds are becoming familiar with Christian talk. Repentance, born-again and salvation are no longer expressions used by the saved alone. Even the man on the street is familiar with them. Songs are more popular if they contain a sacred thought. While men seem quite willing to approve religion **at a distance,** talk of Christ's claim upon their lives is a different matter.

It is because of this, that God has given us the unique tool of psychology. With insight-skill, the smoke screen can be pushed aside and the unsaved man exposed to his miserable condition. Instead of letting men hide behind their excuses to escape in ignorance, we now have the means of brushing aside their defenses and bringing them face to face with Christ. This does not trespass the work of the Holy Spirit. It is a human effort surrendered to the Lord. It is as though we, with human hands, were to take a man by the shoulders and hold him in place so that he must look at Christ. **The Holy Spirit's job is to make Christ real. Psychology's job is to make men FACE HIM.** These are **separate** works. The decision a man makes is his own, of course. For neither psychology nor the Holy Spirit can interfere with that. God has ordained it so.

WHAT ABOUT REPENTANCE?

There are two basic approaches to the development of soul-winning plans; one positive and one negative. The **negative** approach emphasizes the fact that all men are **sinners** and must repent of their sins. The **positive** approach emphasizes the **gift** of God and that men must receive Christ. The Encounter-Method is patterned after the positive approach and focuses on the truth that men must **have** Christ in order to be saved. That man is a terrible sinner who must forsake sin is not the central theme.

In this method of soul-winning, the **Person** of Jesus is the central theme. Christ is offered as the Supreme Gift and the prospects are made to behold Him. This is not to say, however, that repentance is not a part of the experience. To be sure it is, for there can be no genuine salvation without repentance. The difference lies in the **means of securing** the repentance.

● What is repentance? Repentance simply means the **turning from** something (or someone) and the **turning to** something (or someone) else. **The act of turning is the repentance.** Being sorry for sins is **not** repentance. It is merely a **means** or method of securing it. Paul, for example, wrote to the Corinthians, **"Now I rejoice, not that I made you sorry, but that ye were made sorry unto repentance."** It is even clearer in the Amplified New Testament;

118

"Yet I am glad now, not because you were pained, but because you were pained unto repentance (that turned you to God); for you felt a grief such as God meant you to feel . . . " (2 Cor. 7:9).

Notice that the sorrow and the repentance are **two separate things** here. The sorrow produced the repentance. And Paul was able to accomplish it by means of a fierce letter that pointed up their evils. Then he continued his thought in the next verse.

 "For godly grief and the pain that God is permitted to direct, produce a repentance that leads and contributes to salvation . . . " (2 Cor. 7:10 A. N. T.).

Through the means of the letter, the Corinthians **changed their minds** about Paul and reversed their stand with respect to godly living.

Repentance is not limited to the salvation experience alone. A man can repent of a business deal. He does this when he changes his mind about a proposition. Judas, you recall, was involved in a business deal amounting to thirty pieces of silver. The Scripture records his repentance. But notice the kind it was. No sooner had he betrayed the Lord than he began to suffer the scorn and condemnation of his fellows. He then regretted that he had entered into the bargain;

 "Then Judas, which betrayed Him, when he saw that he was condemned (by the others), repented himself (within himself and changed his mind) and brought again the thirty pieces of silver to the chief priests and elders" (Matt. 27:3).

He found himself in a terrible plight when the Jewish leaders refused to call off the deal. He then went out and hanged himself. The point to notice is that Judas' repentance was **toward the priests.** He was **not repenting toward God.** He merely changed his mind about the proposition. Had he repented toward God it would have been a different story. He would have been forgiven, and quickly too. Of course God foreknew he would not and even the Scriptures foretold the event. Paul makes sure that his readers understand that it is **"repentance TOWARD God and faith TOWARD our Lord Jesus Christ"** that delivers (Acts 20:21). **Repentance by itself means nothing.**

In the salvation experience there can be repentance without a bit of sorrow for sins. In fact, there can be **great joy**—joy which comes through beholding Christ and His promises. This joy can also produce repentance. People saved in this way, turn to Jesus because of the joy that is set before them. It is unfortunate when workers confuse sorrow with repentance. **Sorrow is not repentance at all,** but simply one means of bringing it about. Joy and the promise of blessings are other means.

Now it is easier to see the two approaches. Sorrow, with tears over sin, is a **negative** approach to repentance, while the offer of Christ is **positive.** The **turning** is the repentance regardless of what it takes to effect it. The **negative** approach deals with the "wages of sin" and focuses the prospect's attention on his terrible plight. Many evangelists favor this approach because it is dramatic, emotional and effective for pulpitry. How alarming can be their cry, "Don't you dare leave this tent or auditorium tonight in your condition. A car could hit you and send you into a godless eternity!" And then, many great soul-winners of the past also favored this method.

But the **positive** approach deals primarily with the "gift of God is eternal life" and focuses the prospect on God's marvelous offer. True, it is less emotional, at least it is generally presented that way. Yet it is positive and holds out the promise of undreamed blessing. This author favors the positive approach for work at the **personal** level, yet recognizing the value of the negative approach at the **mass** level. Negativism is not popular today. Those who would deal with their friends and neighbors and continue to live before them should avoid being branded with social stigma. One using the positive approach finds a larger circle of acceptance and therefore a wider door of opportunity.

• It is easy to see the positive approach in other areas of life. Parents, for instance, often employ the positive approach in getting children to change their minds about something. A favorite way of getting a child to abandon an objectionable thing is to offer him something better to take its place. For example, he may be reluctant to go to bed, but promise of a trip to Grandma's tomorrow, may induce him to change his mind (repent). It's true that the negative approach is also necessary with children. And when it is, it usually takes the form of a spanking or scolding. That certainly places the emphasis on the child's evils, doesn't it?

The one who sees an infant playing dangerously near the edge of a cliff must decide which approach is best for saving the child. He can shout a warning (negative) which might frighten the child into a fatal move, or, he can hold up a toy or candy (positive). Either could be effective, perhaps, in securing his turning (repentance) away from danger to safety.

• In spite of the clear distinction I have made here between the two approaches, both elements are present to some degree in all soul-winning. It is really a matter of **emphasis** that makes the difference. The one using the negative approach must still introduce Christ or there is no salvation. The one using the positive approach must point out the fact of sin or there is no need for a Savior. The whole matter is nicely illustrated by the figure of a "teeter-totter." Pressing down on one end of the board doesn't get rid of the other end. It is still there, but one end is receiving the greater pressure (emphasis). It is the turning of the board at the center axis that pictures repentance. The ends represent the two approaches.

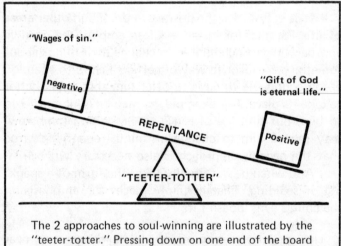

The 2 approaches to soul-winning are illustrated by the "teeter-totter." Pressing down on one end of the board doesn't get rid of the other end. It is still there, but one end is receiving the greater pressure (emphasis). The turning of the board at the center axis pictures repentance. The ends represent the 2 approaches. The Encounter-Method uses the positive approach.

What is generally missed in discussions of repentance is that repentance itself is an **automatic feature** of either approach. When a man **turns from** anything, he automatically **turns to** something else. Conversely, when a man turns **to** Christ **he has to turn from** whatever object previously held his trust. Repentance may be harder to see in the positive approach, but it is there. There can be no salvation without it. One cannot trust himself and Christ at the same time. He has to turn from one to the other. The one who places his trust in Jesus, **automatically lets go** of the former object of his faith. If he hasn't, he has not truly received Christ as his Savior.

● With these truths in mind, the greatest advantage of the positive approach may now be mentioned—it's **simplicity!** All that is involved is a simple introduction to Jesus. This feature makes it easy for people of all ages. Even little ones can learn to introduce someone. The negative approaches, which deal with people's doubts, fears, and objections, require a host of Bible verses and usually some form of worker's **catalogue.** These are intended to deal with the myriad problems and questions that arise. Yet, after one has answered all the questions and objections, he still must introduce his prospect to the Lord. **Why not start there to begin with?** It only takes four verses to make the introduction—and the introduction situation is nearly always the same.

Chapter Ten

Do I Have To Try To Win Everybody?

"Jesus said to them, 'Come with me and I will make you fishers of men.' " (Matt. 4:19 NEB)

THE TWO TYPES OF SOUL-WINNING

Once armed with a soul-winning plan and trained to use it, Christians are sometimes agonized by the question: "Now that I have acquired a successful plan, am I expected to corner every person I meet and confront him with Christ?" The wise teacher replies with an unequivocal "No!" To be under such fearful compulsion is more than most Christians can bear. A knowledge of the two types of soul-winning provides a healthy answer to that disturbing question.

There are two methods of soul-winning: the **active-aggressive** type, where one makes a point of contacting people deliberately in order to present the Lord; and the **passive** type, where one waits for the Lord to provide a clear-cut opening. In the former you go to people with your message and in the latter they come to you for spiritual help. By far, most Christians prefer the latter. **Both types** were used by our Lord. In John Chapter Three, it was Nicodemus who came to Him seeking help, but in Chapter Four, He confronted the woman at the well.

In John Chapter Four, Jesus confronted the woman at the well. In this case He used the **active-aggressive** type of soul-winning.

Wise Christians prepare themselves for both types of soul-winning, employing a simple principle of expediency for determining which method is best for a given situation. The principle is this:

Where it is important to have social acceptability, always use the passive type.

The reason is simple. The gospel, **aggressively presented**, will always divide the presenter from the world. There can be no social acceptability when Christ's challenge is forcibly introduced. He is still the divider of men and His Word is resented and rejected by most of mankind.

1. THE PASSIVE TYPE OF SOUL-WINNING

Experience shows that on the job and in fraternal gatherings, social acceptability is important and should be preserved. The Christian can **live** his message in those places where he cannot **declare it**. Outspoken boldness would isolate him and he would no longer have any ministry at all. Particularly on the job, one should discreetly use the **passive** approach. This type has two steps:

a. Subtly **identify** yourself as a Christian. This can be done with the **lips** by offering guarded remarks such as, **"As a Christian I feel that . . . ,"** or, **"Lord willing I will do thus and so . . ."** Your **actions**, such as reading your Testament at the lunch hour or having it carefully placed on your desk fairly scream a loud identification. These clues, without a word to anyone, mark you as a man or woman of God.

b. God does the rest. Those in need will seek you out for a secluded interview. Then you can deal with them without fear of stirring antagonism. When troubled ones bring their questions, you can wisely answer, **"Since YOU have mentioned it . . . ,"** or, **"Now that YOU have brought it up, I wonder if anyone has asked concerning your interest in spiritual things?"** This, you see, throws the responsibility for the interview upon them. No one can accuse you of cramming religion down the throats of the office force and it

126

will keep you out of trouble with your employer.

2. THE ACTIVE TYPE OF SOUL-WINNING

Life is filled with opportunities for the **aggressive** type soul-winning too. The car makes a fine place to deal with high school lads seeking rides home from school. Many unsaved people go to religious meetings able to resist the **public** challenge of the evangelist, but here's where the aggressive technique pays off. The **private** challenge of Jesus' claim cannot be avoided. Home visitation programs provide unlimited opportunities (See **VISITATION MADE EASY**). The salesman calling at our door might well be sent by God and in need of this approach. Our neighbors make excellent prospects, too.

We give our best service when ready with both types and guided by the principle of **social** acceptability. This is the key. Social acceptability is important to those who want to **live Christ** before others as well as proclaim the way to God. It is Christian wisdom to select the right type for any situation which will not interfere with your being a **living** representative of Jesus Christ. The lived message carries more power. Then, in those places where you do not have to **demonstrate** your message, the aggressive type is proper. Now we can answer our question better . . .

NO, BUT YOU SHOULD BE
READY TO WIN ANYBODY.

Nothing is more distressing to the trained soul-winner than to have a choice opportunity to talk with someone about Christ and find he does not have a **BEGINNING TO LIVE** in his pocket. Since there is no way for us to know when the Holy Spirit will grant us an opportunity to introduce someone to Jesus, we must always be prepared. So make sure you never leave the house without first checking to see that your tools are handy. The Lord counsels,

 ". . . Come after Me [as disciples] —letting Me be your Guide, follow Me—and I will make you fishers of men!" (Matt. 4:19 A.N.T.)

If we are to follow Him in this call, we must have our "tackle" ready for the moment He needs us. What an awful feeling to think of the "ones that got away."

Illus: You hear a siren coming down your street. The paramedics stop at the house next door. You know your neighbor has a weak heart, he's had attacks in the past. You also know he's heard the gospel, but has put off receiving Christ. When you get there, the medics have him on the sofa, awaiting the ambulance. He's conscious. He gestures to you. He wants to say something. As you reach his side, he says, "I'm afraid this'll be my last one. I don't want to go to hell. Help me!"

Would it be hard to bring such a person to Jesus? This is a case where ANYONE could lead him to Christ—if he knew how. This is why it pays to be equipped with a plan and know how to use it. You may dread the idea of confronting another person with Christ, but in such a moment as this you could easily do it—if you knew how. How embarrassing it would be to have to say to your neighbor, "I'll have to get the pastor . . . ," when God has made you the man on the scene. Armed with this plan and the booklet or Testament, any Christian could serve the Lord nobly in such a situation.

Illus: Sometimes a little job started in the back yard

can end with an over-the-fence conversation with a neighbor, or, what first appears to be a trip to the store might prove to be a soul-winning expedition if we are equipped for it.

Sometimes a little job started in the back yard can end with an over-the-fence conversation with a neighbor who shows interest in spiritual things. You'll want to be prepared.

Illus: Some find it good to keep an extra Testament or **BEGINNING TO LIVE** in the car just in case that lad on the way home from High School has been selected by the Holy Spirit. Again it might be someone you meet in the parking lot while your wife is inside shopping. The car makes a wonderful place for fishing. Here the worker has all the privacy he needs.

Just as the frontiersmen of early days felt half-clothed without their "six-guns" strapped to their side, so ought the soul-winner to feel naked and incomplete without his tools. It should be a rule to go no place without them. What a shame to let golden opportunities slip by simply because we haven't taken time to be prepared. Therefore we can observe this. **The more prepared we are, the more likely is the Holy Spirit to open the opportunity to us.**

Just as the frontiersmen of
early days felt half-clothed
without their "six-guns"
strapped to their side,
so ought the soul-winner to
feel naked and incomplete
without his tools.

THE PROOF OF THE PUDDING

Now that you have read the plan, don't you think you could be a soul-winner? Wouldn't you like to try? Simply become familiar with the four verses, learn the transition lines and then practice with a friend. In no time you will be ready for "active duty." Why not get started this coming Sunday? Speak to your pastor or some close friend and see what could be done about starting a class in your church. Show him the teacher's book **SOUL-WINNING CLASSES MADE EASY**. It's fun when others join in. Soon the whole group could be in the swing of winning men for Christ. It could even be the beginning of revival in your fellowship.

Naturally, Satan will be upset. So don't pay any attention to his whispered, "I'm not called to win souls," or, "That's what preachers are for," or, "I don't have enough education." He will try to plant all sorts of doubts in your mind. He panics when Christians begin to stir in this fashion.

This book and a little practice can be your seminary for soul-winning. B.D. and Ph.D. degrees are not necessary for introducing men to Jesus. Present yourself and your plan to the Lord and see if this isn't so. That is the real test anyway. You will find, that once you get started, it is easy, it is thrilling and it is fun!

Chapter Eleven

Too Scared
To Try?

*". . . but courage! The victory is mine; I have conquered
the world."* (John 16:33 NEB)

Not everyone reading this book will put it to use immediately. Some are going to be too scared to try. I understand that. We are not all made alike. Some of us are
bold, others are timid and shy. Certainly those with
salesman type personalities will have no trouble putting
this skill into operation. Neither would those who are
meeting the public in connection with their occupations.
But there are brethren who are scared to death at the
thought of a soul-winning encounter.

Some years ago the Lord made it plain to me that
only a certain percentage of believers would be able to
learn this plan and put it to use. The others just wouldn't
have the necessary personality strengths. After all, it is
not the easiest thing in the world to approach a stranger
and:

1. Involve him in a spiritual conversation when his mind is on other things.

2. Use God's Word so skillfully that it brings the conviction of sin.

3. Shift him to a different emotion as you explain how Christ is the answer to his need.

4. Escort his thinking to the place where he is aware of Christ knocking at his heart's door. This can be a shock.

5. Press him to do something with the Lord Jesus, one way or another.

The soul-winning plan I have presented in this book is easy to use **if** you have the social strengths necessary. If you don't, it could be a nightmare. To go from silence (and most Christians are silent) to soul-winning—**in one jump**—can be a terrifying experience for those who are shy. In fact, it is usually impossible.

So what should they do?

CONSIDER WITNESSING

Those who cannot immediately use the plan of this book as soul-winners, should consider witnessing. They should serve the Lord as witnesses until they have gained the strength they need to be soul-winners. There are all kinds of ways to witness ranging from leaving a tract in secret to telling someone what Jesus means to you. A person can move gradually between those two extremes until he finally has the strength to lead someone to Christ. Then it will be easy for him to use the plan in this book.

WE'RE ALL CALLED TO BE WITNESSES

For over twenty-five years I've been in the business of teaching people how to witness. Never have I found a person who couldn't do it—once he learned how.

The first thing you need to know is this: witnessing and soul-winning are two different things.

When I speak of witnessing, I **DO NOT** mean confronting people with Christ and asking them to receive Him as Savior. Having read this book, you know that's soul-winning. The average Christian doesn't have the strength for that, at least not at first. But when it comes to letting others know ABOUT Jesus, that is another matter. Any believer can do that—with know-how.

IT HELPS TO SEE THE DIFFERENCE

When I explain the difference between soul-winning and witnessing, you'll agree that witnessing is for you. The idea is not nearly so frightening when you know what is involved. To behold the difference clearly, come with me to a courtroom.

The judge calls the **witness** to the stand. After he's sworn in, he makes statements from his personal knowledge. He is not on trial. He simply tells what he knows. That's all. He doesn't have to convince anyone of anything. Once he's made his statement, he's all through and steps down. His task is to supply information only. He tells what he knows and that's it.

The **prosecutor**, on the other hand, behaves differently. He doesn't take the stand. He's a lawyer, skilled in handling people, obtaining from them what he wants. Then he uses that information to prove his point. With clever words and techniques he seeks to convince the judge or jury. Everything he does is aimed at getting a decision in his favor.

● **The soul-winner is like a prosecuting attorney.** He employs a skillful approach to the prospect. Using calcu-

134

lated phrases, he extracts information from his prospect and then uses that information to bring him face to face with Christ. With careful timing he moves up to the crisis point and presses for a decision. Everything he does and says is geared to getting his man to DO SOMETHING with Jesus. If he does it right, there is no way for a prospect to avoid a face to face encounter with the Lord. You can see that takes skill and confidence.

Witnessing, is not like that at all. **Once a witness has passed on his information to a prospect, whether by words from his lips or by means of a tract, his work is done.** When believers do not know this, they are inclined to think witnessing means soul-winning. No wonder they panic when someone suggests they witness for the Lord.

Have I said Christians should NOT win souls? No. If a believer has natural gifts that make it easy for him to approach people with persuasive charm, he should be a soul-winner. Such Christians are often salesmen or public workers. Equip them with a systematic approach for presenting Christ and they're instant soul-winners. But for the rest, however, soul-winning is still in the future. They must first **START OUT as witnesses to gain the necessary strength and boldness.** Later, perhaps, when they have learned to move in the Holy Spirit, and enjoy approaching people for Christ, they could consider soul-winning. But for the moment they should relax in the Lord's words . . . "Ye shall be WITNESSES unto Me" (Acts 1:8).

IT HELPS TO KNOW THIS

I had just finished a soul-winning message in a fundamental church, when a tearful lady rushed forward to speak to me. She was nervous, perspiring. Her hands twisted a knotted handkerchief. She was visibly upset.

"Dr. Lovett, I'm ashamed to say this, but I can't witness for the Lord. I don't know how to win souls. And I'm sure I couldn't do it even if I knew how."

"Forget soul-winning," I said to her. **"It has nothing to do with you right now. Why don't you consider becoming a witness. Perhaps later on you can think about winning souls."**

At first she was puzzled by my words. Like so many, she thought she couldn't witness for Christ without being a soul-winner. When I explained the difference, her face brightened. Her shoulders dropped in relief. You could see the tension fade from her body. Those few words removed an awful burden from her soul. Then I gave her some easy steps for getting started. That lady went away rejoicing.

It was to meet this need that the Lord gave me the Ladder-Method of witnessing.

136

THE LADDER-METHOD OF WITNESSING

Can a man go from the ground to the roof of his house in one jump? Hardly. But there's nothing to keep him from getting a ladder which will allow him to cover the same distance in easy steps. Well the same thing can be done with witnessing. A shy Christian can use a **ladder** to get from the easiest type of witnessing to aggressive soul-winning. Yet, if he tried to make it in one jump, it would be impossible. He can't do that anymore than a man can jump from the ground to the roof of his home. But when that distance is broken up into steps which he can climb, one rung at a time, it becomes simple.

Just as a man cannot go from the ground to the roof of a building without a ladder, neither can a Christian go from silence to aggressive soul-winning without a plan which breaks the distance up into easy steps.

The Ladder-Method of witnessing presents a series of graded actions the shy Christian can accomplish in easy steps. He begins by secretly leaving tracts in phone booths, restaurants, etc., and eases his way up through harder actions until he reaches the highest form of witnessing—telling someone what Jesus means to him. There's no hurry in reaching the top rung. He stays at each level until he is comfortable in the action. When he feels his strength has increased, he moves to the next rung. In this way the witnessing threat comes in doses he can handle.

In time, the witness can look back down the ladder to see how far he has come. He gets a tremendous thrill out of doing things for Christ he never thought he could do— and with such ease. That's what a ladder does for people. After he has climbed through all ten steps, he will then have the strength to be a soul-winner. He will also know how to work with the Holy Spirit—**at close range**. That's one of the precious things you pick up when you become serious about witnessing. Once you have the confidence that working with the Spirit brings, you'll be ready to use the soul-winning plan in this book.

WITNESSING MADE EASY

See that book on the left? It's titled **WITNESSING MADE EASY**. It presents the LADDER-METHOD in great detail, showing you how to get started and climb up the ladder one step at a time. It has 256 pages of pictures, actions, dialogues, and know-how. On the first two rungs, you have NO contact with people at all. This means there is no interpersonal threat. You begin by leaving tracts secretly. They have to be secret because you will be conducting experiments with the Holy Spirit to sample His power.

The first thing you learn in this approach is that it is the Spirit of God Who makes witnessing easy. I know you agree with that idea IN THEORY. But wait until you meet it in PRACTICE! Wow! I assure you it is thrilling to experience His power IN EACH ACTION STEP.

Let me be frank with you. I'm after soul-winners. But I know I'm not going to get too many without providing some way for the shy Christian to develop the strengths necessary for the soul-winning encounter. If you tend to be timid or reluctant to press the claims of Christ on people, why not give thought to witnessing? I guarantee you'll be able to use the Encounter-Method after you complete the ten steps.

Why have I spoken so earnestly about witnessing? It's a wonderful form of insurance. Some of you are going to try soul-winning and get discouraged. Others will learn the plan only to find they don't have the strength to use it. Don't you think it is exciting to learn there is a way to acquire the strength you need? Of course. Therefore if you have any doubt as to your ability to use the EN-COUNTER METHOD of soul-winning, you can insure yourself against failure with the LADDER-METHOD of witnessing.

I don't want to lose any of you. I hope that those who need to, will get a copy of **WITNESSING MADE EASY** and protect themselves against failure. Beyond that, write to me. Let us get your name before our weekly prayer group to seek the power of the Holy Spirit on your behalf. Since this is PERSONAL CHRIS-TIANITY, you can write to us for personal help.

And now may the Lord grant you the thrill of winning souls to lay at His feet in that day!

MARANATHA! (O Lord Come!)

C. S. Lovett

139

TOOLS FOR THE TEACHER

No. 202-SOUL-WINNING CLASSES MADE EASY — By C. S. Lovett
$1.75 Teacher's guide for SOUL-WINNING MADE EASY. Shows how the author teaches soul-winning. 6 1-hour sessions. (80 pages, paper)

No. 204-SOUL-WINNING FILMSTRIP & RECORD — By C. S. Lovett
$6.00 Motivates your church to sign up for a soul-winning class. Takes 15 minutes. Full color 35 mm filmstrip, 33 1/3 rpm record, instructions.

No. 211-SOUL-WINNING AWARD CERTIFICATE — By C. S. Lovett
25 for $1.50 Given upon completion of soul-winning lab class. (8½" x 11", 2 colors, pebbletone finish, shrinkwrapped in 25's)

No. 212-SOUL-WINNING WORKSHOP FOLDER — By C. S. Lovett
25 for 50¢ Overview of course, registration form. (size 5½" x 8½", 4 pages, shrinkwrapped in 25's)

No. 213-SOUL-WINNING LAB CARD — By C. S. Lovett **25 for 50¢**
Soul-winning plan in 3"x 5" outline card, shrinkwrapped in 25's.

No. 214-SOUL-WINNING FEAR CERTIFICATE — By C. S. Lovett
25 for 50¢ Believer's inactive permit signed by Satan. Challenges indifferent students. (size 4¼" x 5½", shrinkwrapped in 25's)

PERSONAL CHRISTIANITY

BOX 549, BALDWIN PARK,
CALIFORNIA 91706
(213) 338-7333

SINCE 1951

QUICK ORDER FORM

PRINT PLAINLY SO PRAYER GROUP CAN PROPERLY READ YOUR NAME. | 7201

NAME_____
EACH TIME YOU ORDER, PLEASE USE EXACT SAME NAME

ADDRESS_____

CITY_____ STATE_____ ZIP_____

ITEM NO.	TITLE	HOW MANY	COST EACH	TOTAL AMOUNT

CLIP AND MAIL TODAY!

DISCOUNT SCHEDULE		
DISCOUNT SCHEDULE if your order totals: $15.00–$24.99 **subtract $1.50** $25.00–$49.99 **subtract $5.00** $50.00 or more **subtract 25%**	**TOTAL ORDER**	
	☞ **LESS DISCOUNT**	
	NET AFTER DISCOUNT	
SPECIAL POSTAGE ☐ SPECIAL HANDLING ☐ SPECIAL DELIVERY ☐ AIR MAIL ☐ AIR MAIL-SPEC DEL	**CALIFORNIA** RESIDENTS ONLY ADD 6% SALES TAX	
	HELP ON POSTAGE	
	OFFERING—help with free literature distribution	
Check box and enclose extra postage for above services. Amount enclosed determines shipping method.	**TOTAL AMOUNT ENCLOSED**	

142

RECORD FOR PRAYER AND FOLLOW-UP

*"you who are my joy in this life and my crown
in the next"* (Phil. 4:1 Lovett's Lights)

NAME_____

ADDRESS_____

CITY_____

STATE_____ ZIP_____

WHERE SAVED_____

DATE_____

FOLLOW-UP_____

_____

_____

_____

_____

_____

_____

_____

REMARKS_____

_____

_____

RECORD FOR PRAYER AND FOLLOW-UP

"you who are my joy in this life and my crown in the next" (Phil. 4:1 Lovett's Lights)

NAME_____

ADDRESS_____

CITY_____

STATE_____ ZIP_____

WHERE SAVED_____

DATE_____

FOLLOW-UP_____

_____

_____

_____

_____

_____

_____

REMARKS_____

_____

_____